Bill DeWees

HOW TO START AND BUILD A
6 FIGURE
VOICE OVER BUSINESS

Set Your VO Career On *Fire!*

DeWees, Bill. How to Start and Build a 6 Figure Voice Business (Set Your VO Career on Fire!)

ISBN: 978-0-9886769-0-9

Copyright © Bill DeWees Media

2013 All rights reserved

First published in 2013

Interior layout: Stanley Dumanig

Contents

FREE OFFER

FREE OFFER for YOU as the owner of this book!

To get my audio program "Seven Secrets to a 6 Figure Voice Over Income"

Just go to: http://goo.gl/U1STb

You can download it RIGHT NOW!

What are you waiting for????

FREE OFFER

This page is intentionally left blank.

Chapter I

Introduction - Voice Over Talent + Business Consultant

There is simply no better way to learn than hearing a seasoned expert speak. This book came about when Fred Gleeck interviewed me, Bill DeWees, and we recorded it. Honestly, the result is nothing short of a clear blueprint for your own voice over business.

As you read this book, you will learn everything you need to know to get started and to succeed in the voice over business. I am a working voice over talent, and I know my stuff. I show you some history, the current market reality, and a glimpse of your own future, if you choose to take on the challenge.

Welcome to my world, and my current reality. How To Start And Build A Six Figure Voice Over Business is my real experience, and now it can be yours as well.

The truth is there are quite a few books out there on the subject of voice over. Perhaps you are wondering why you should listen to me, and what sets me apart from other voice over talent coaches who set about to teach others the business.

Frankly, what I bring to the table is unique. There are other voice over talent coaches, plenty of them, but most operate without the training, teaching and business background I enjoy. You might say I have the benefit of knowing the best of both worlds... voice talent and business skills.

I'm a former college professor with an MBA degree. I taught marketing at the post graduate level, and I have worked as a marketing consultant and business consultant in a consulting firm in Chicago. I have worked with small- to mid-sized businesses and helped them understand what was going on in their businesses, and how to chart a course towards the future.

I also have an extensive background in radio broadcasting. I understand what it takes to get out there on the street to market myself, and then get out there on the air and perform. I've done all this with low budgets to no budgets at all for marketing, so I have real life expertise in the trenches. I excel in helping voice over talent get started, when there is not much money for self promotion.

This book concentrates on two basic areas, both of which are critical to your success. First is the performance side of the voice over business - how to do the actual voice over work in terms of performance. Second, but even more important, is the business side - marketing yourself to get clients, to generate work and to build a six figure income.

You may have already read and heard volumes of material written and recorded about how to be a great performer. Even though there is a lot of good material available, what I add to the conversation is completely unique, and it can make or break your career in voice over.

Let's start with two hard, cold facts to absorb and believe right now: 1) Talent isn't hard to find; 2) Talent that makes money is very hard to find.

Once you consider these facts, you are in a better position to understand why I am so unique in the marketplace. I help voice talent bridge the big gap between performance and profit. I can do this because I do it myself every day. I am a successful voice over talent and I am here to tell you how to do what I do every day.

I've been building my voice over business for about seven years now, and my income speaks for itself. I have a system that can work for you, too. It can help you achieve success, because voice over is a way to create sustainable and growing income. It is not hit or miss, especially if you follow my system.

Sadly, for most voice talent a decent income is always hit or miss. You may get a big job now, but it may be another few months or years before you get your next big job. When I started, my first year in the voice over business, I earned approximately $7,200. I have to tell you, that was a rough first year... but by the end of it, I began to average more than $2,000 a week.

If you do the math the way we do it in post graduate classes, I was actually at a six figure income by the end of my first year.

My second year was about $104,000; my third year was $112,000; I believe my fourth year it was in the low $120,000s, then I quickly broke $130,000. Last year I made approximately $150,000, and right now I'm averaging close to $5,000 a week. My income from voice over work will be right at $250,000 this year.

If those numbers sound good to you, read on and find out how to achieve them for yourself.

Chapter 2

What is Voice Over?

To define it simply, I would say voice is any recording, using your voice, for the purpose of communicating a message. That's it. Voice over is voice recording, in its simplest and broadest sense.

From there, it could take the form of a commercial for radio, television, or internet media. It could be a movie trailer, a radio promo, an "on-hold" telephone system recording, a YouTube video, a podcast, or any other purpose. This list could go on and on, but it conveys the idea of using your voice to communicate a message.

Let me tell you one thing voice over is NOT. It is not about having a big, booming announcer voice. Those days are over. The sound of authority is no longer a stereotype.

In the old days, the announcer sound was based on a military model, and it was often the way parents communicated with their children, too. It was understood to be the voice of authority, in the media, and in the home as well. The sound of authority, the sound of a person telling you what to do was big, bold and rather obnoxious.

These days, listeners are turned off by the announcer approach. It doesn't work in the media and it rarely works in the home. What people want now is the sound of a voice they can relate to, that they can hear and understand clearly, with a comfortable familiarity that resonates with them.

To me, voice over is basically telling a story. High quality voice over is telling a story well, so it is heard and understood by the listener.

Whether you are telling a story, describing an e-learning program, narrating an audio book or reading a commercial, you are telling a story. When you become skilled at connecting with people and telling a story, that is when you become a successful voice over talent.

One of the amazing things about success in the voice over industry is that you absolutely do not need a great voice.

Let me repeat, you do not need a great voice to be successful in voice over.

Success in voice over is less about what you sound like and more about what you can do with your voice. Success is about how you connect with other people. In the old days, you had to sound big and bold to be authoritative. Today you have to sound friendly and familiar. You have to sound like a person the listener can instantly like.

Companies that pay for voice over talent hire people who can connect with other people. The most important thing you can do to develop your talent is to change your thinking now. Voice over success is all about communicating. Your success will ultimately be based on how well you relate and communicate. It is not based on any attempt to speak with a flawless radio announcer voice.

Some of the best communicators do not speak perfectly at all. I am thinking about Barbara Walters. She has an obvious speech impediment, but she has had a long career as a highly paid, very successful media professional because she knows how to communicate with people.

Barbara Walters is not a voice over talent, but the same rules essentially apply to voice over talent. At the end of the day it's not about your voice. Of course, it doesn't hurt to have a nice voice, and there are a few jobs that call for a great authoritative announcer, but those jobs are few and far between. The majority of hires have a guy or girl next door type of voice.

You want to sound like a person who listeners can like, and can relate to as they listen to stories. This is the basic voice quality you want to develop in order to achieve lasting success.

Almost anybody who can tell a story can do voice overs. Most people who get into this business have a mistaken idea about what it is. We all start out thinking we need a big booming voice. But in reality, NOTHING could be further from the truth. If you are a parent who has told stories to your children, or a teacher or a grandparent who has read stories to children, you can record voice overs.

Ladies and Gentlemen, surprising as it may seem, parenting and grand parenting provide excellent qualifications for a voice over career. And if you are a school teacher, you are already a professional communicator because you know how to speak to an audience. And I love to work with salespeople because most salespeople are great storytellers and also great communicators.

One of my most successful students is a pastor. Now he's a guy who knows how to tell a story! He's very homespun, very down to earth, and he's been quite effective using his natural tone in the voice over marketplace. Counselors and others who listen and talk for their living are well suited to explore a career in voice over.

While we are busting some myths here, let me mention another one. All voice over jobs are not created equal. Most of us think of radio commercials, television commercials and movie trailers, or what I call high profile jobs, as typical voice over jobs. They are not typical, they are rare.

Picture all types of voice over jobs as an iceberg. If you simply look at the tip of the iceberg, where it comes up and out of the water, there you will find the radio and television commercials and the movie trailers. But beneath the surface, somewhat hidden where the casual observer may fail to see what is going on, is a huge mass of work. There are millions of dollars waiting to be earned recording audio books alone. So, let's talk about audio books for a moment.

Did you know there are approximately 100,000 traditional books published every year? Approximately 5% of those become audio books as well. Amazon is a major a player in the audio book market now because they own Audible.com, probably the largest online seller of audio books. Amazon and Audible are dedicated to increasing the audio book marketplace. They intend to build their market by recording books as audio books, and doing so with as many books as possible.

Audio Creative Exchange, ACX.com, is a marketplace for audio book producers, authors and voice over talent. It is already huge, and it's growing. Audio books are a rapidly growing market. A lot of people don't realize that because so many people record at home now, making YouTube videos and MP3 audio recordings. How many kids are in their bedrooms creating really great stuff now, in terms of video and audio production?

But, many of those efforts need voice overs. That's the good news. I do tons of 90- to 120-second long videos explaining products for companies that require voice overs. I have done in-store commercials for Sears. That's an example of new ways and new places voice overs are needed now.

I've done in-store riding mower spots, the ones you see in specialty kiosks. I record a lot of in-store kiosk videos for LG Electronics, too. Think about it, whenever you go to Best Buy or Costco or Walmart and notice videos playing, remember that somebody had to record the voice over. The sound of your voice could be filling up retail chain stores, too.

Now, let's touch on e-learning because I worked in that area prior to getting into voice overs. E-learning classes are cheaper than sending people into classrooms. Most of it requires voice over. There is more e-learning being created than we can fathom because it saves time and money for companies and for their employees.

Voice over is an unlimited career now. If you can talk and tell a story that conveys a message, you can produce voice overs. If you can learn to market yourself, you can have a successful career producing your voice overs.

Chapter 3

What Can You Earn?

This will probably be the most popular chapter in my book, How To Start And Build A Six Figure Voice Over Business. But, in a way, it is one of the most difficult topics.

The reason is because there are really two questions, not one. The first question is, "What CAN I earn?" And the second question is, "What DO people earn?"

What can you earn? Well, truthfully, the sky is the limit. There are certainly voice over talent making seven figure incomes. However, you can probably count those people on your fingers and toes. It's not a huge population. Very few voice over talent are earning seven figure incomes, and most of those big earners live in New York City and Los Angeles. They are available to do movie trailer work and national television work. Voice over is very competitive in those spaces. But there is a much larger group of people earning six figures. I have shown you that a six figure income is not only possible, but it is a reality for me.

But honestly, most people who call themselves voice over talent don't even earn a part-time income. That may sound somewhat shocking, but it comes from my experience talking to a lot of people over the years. It is nearly impossible to get reliable statistics on part-time voice over income, so most of what I'm sharing is anecdotal.

One statistic is available online. CareerBuilder.com comes out with lists of annual salaries, and in 2010 it listed voice actors as having an average annual salary of $47,000. But I take that figure with a grain of salt because the truth is many people are not making nearly that much.

It's not that they cannot make $47,000, but with their marketing skills and persistence level they are making less. Sometimes I wonder if the seven figure folks skew the average for the rest of us. CBS also did a salary poll a couple years ago and reported that voice over talent makes an average of $47,700 a year.

The Bureau of Labor Statistics recently reported that the median income for beginners in the voice talent industry is $16.59 an hour.

But I'd like to turn the tide here, and start to give you the good news, and you will soon see why I'm so excited. Besides the fact that I'm able to make good money doing voice overs, I know other people who make good money doing it, too. Many of those people are actors, they're "creatives". By this I mean they treat their voice over business more like an art than a business.

Maybe this sounds biased or opinionated to you. But remember, I am a talent and also a business man, and so I operate on both sides of the fence. That gives me a perspective that is allowing me to succeed, and to help others succeed as well.

What I have discovered in the past several years of working in the voice over business is that some world class talent – voices you would recognize - are living from job to job. This is a little bit shocking, too, but big name voice over talent may work a huge job that pays $10,000, but it eventually comes to an end and so does the money. Even two or three of these big jobs each year only brings in a total income below the poverty level.

One candid conversation I had recently with a guy who has done some pretty high profile voice overs sticks in my mind. He said, "I gotta get a real job. I cannot sustain a living doing what I do."

But again, the problem is simply that most people who get behind a microphone are creative people, they're performers, and they think like performers. If you can make the shift from performer, to business person… or I won't even say shift, I'll just say if you can learn how to be a business person and a marketer, you can succeed.

Fortunately, it is not as complicated as you may think. If you can do that, if you can approach your voice over work as a business, it is reasonable to expect to make $50,000 a year as a voice talent. $50,000 is very reasonable, and it is just the beginning if you choose to follow my system.

At this point you may be wondering if I make more money teaching voice over, or if I am earning most of my income by performing voice overs. While I don't have an exact percentage to give you, I can say that coaching accounts for less than 5% of my total income at this point.

I am a full-time voice talent. I spend the majority of my time behind a microphone. Of course I love coaching and I do it as much as I can, but when a person has a full-time, dedicated profession, that's pretty much it. It's been my experience that most people cannot have two full-time careers at once.

I have to admit it is very frustrating to see other people promoting their voice over training service because they can no longer make a living doing voice overs themselves. The market has changed dramatically since they were making good money as voice talent, so they are coaching to supplement their income. There are some really great coaches out there, and I don't want to demean their efforts at all.

But it frustrates me, too. They may be providing voice coaching, but they are not teaching their students how to market themselves to get the voice over work. If a beginner does not learn both skills, they are doomed to failure.

I say that selling voice over is not much different from selling widgets. Marketing is marketing is marketing. The skill set required is a little bit different, but not the marketing and the business element. If you understand the basic principles of business and marketing, and you are willing to utilize them on a daily basis, you can succeed.

Only a small percentage of my income comes from coaching and training now because I don't have much time to spare from my voice over work. I am a full-time, working, voice over talent.

Some coaches have strong performance skills and some are better coaches than performers. If you are talking to a coach, make sure that person has done exactly what you want to do. If you want to become a great cartoon voice, find somebody who is a great cartoon voice. But, here's a warning in advance…

Be sure you ask how much money that person earns doing cartoon voices because I've talked to people who have worked as big time cartoon voices and right now they aren't earning much money at all. The problem is not because they lack talent. Actually, they ooze talent; the problem is that they don't know how to market themselves today in the current voice over marketplace.

I ask you, how can a voice over coach teach you how to succeed without knowing how to market their talent now?

Chapter 4

The Old Voice Over Model –
A Blast From The Past

This chapter describes how the voice over business used to be, and how it has changed. The old voice over business model is dead and gone. Let's talk about that, about how things used to be, so you can have a better perspective on how things are today.

The voice over business is not the same as it was 15, 20, or 30 years ago. There has been a dramatic change, and that is the crux of the problem for most old-timers in the business. Talent is not enough anymore. Marketing has become as important, or even more important, than talent.

The old voice over model is similar to many other businesses in one significant way. Over the past 10-20 years, the middleman has been squeezed out. Performers can record themselves and promote themselves, and in fact they must do so to survive. Technology has changed everything in voice over, just as it has in other industries.

The middleman, so to speak, used to be the talent agent. The agent was the keeper of the keys. If you didn't have an agent you had no way to find work. Agents are still around now, but there's a big difference. In the past, agents would vet their talent, and they would keep a book of talent. Agents would negotiate on behalf of their talent because they had the power.

Then the internet came along and artists could send audio files directly to clients. That's when clients and artists all began to realize they really didn't need agents. Everything became faster and cheaper, the same things other industries experienced, and the middleman was no longer the keeper of the keys.

Well, at least not entirely. Today, the top commercials and projects are still handled by talent agents because they still have access to the most talent. They still have their little black books of contacts. When you move up in the voice over world, you will want agents to know about you. I have 16 agents myself right now.

Actually, I love agents. I have nothing against agents at all. But, you have to understand in today's marketplace YOU are your best agent. That fact is the hardest thing for old-timers to understand. The gentleman I mentioned earlier, the one who used to do very high profile work, also said, "I heard from my agent maybe once or twice in the last year, and I did an audition or two and then -- nothing."

Back in the day, people waited for their agents to call. These days, agents are not going to call you. Even though I've got 16 agents, if I waited around for them to call me I would go bankrupt. I get some great work from my agents, but not enough to sustain me regularly.

Right now, less than 2% of my income comes from jobs through my agents. This should really help you put the importance of marketing yourself into sharp perspective.

I keep my agents, and I audition for jobs, because usually they are higher profile, better paying jobs. That means I am competing against the best of the best in the voice over industry, the top tier talent. We are all competing against each other. We are all good, but only one person is going to get the job.

But my focus in this book is about 98% of the voice over work available; it's not about the other 2%. So, if you are wondering whether I would advise you to get an agent, I say - go ahead. And congratulations if you can get one, but don't expect it to do anything major for your voice over career. It probably won't.

Let's focus on the new voice over model now. The good news is that companies needing voice over talent can find you online. And although radio and television stations formerly used in-house talent to record, now there are recording houses dedicated to nothing but high volume, low cost radio and television spots.

The bad news is those spots don't pay as much as, say, a national Sears commercial. But, when you get several spots per day, all of a sudden you are earning some real money. I work for quite a few of those recording houses myself. I like to stay diversified and generate income from many different sources.

You might want to think about it like this – don't put all your eggs in one basket. This philosophy has a number of positive benefits. You can keep a steady cash flow going by taking on a lot of smaller jobs. Although my income has trended up over the past seven years, it's amazing how predictable it has become. A steady stream of income is always my goal.

Unlike some of my peers, I don't care to live with insecurity. I hear people say, "I get a job here, I get a job there, but I never know what to expect." At this point in my career I can tell you with great confidence exactly what I'm going to make this week, and what I'm going to make next month.

My secret is my large portfolio. It's like having a mutual fund of clients. Some are big jobs, some are smaller jobs. But I keep in touch with them and I get work from them on a consistent basis.

I remember back when I only dreamed about making $200 a day. That was my goal. If I could do that much, then I could do voice overs full-time. I remember dreaming about that every day and then one day I finally made $200. Then I thought, "Oh, if I could just do this every day for a few months..." I was growing my business because of my marketing efforts. It was not an accident.

Of course my income goal continued to rise, and it continues to rise more and more every day.

One other factor worth mentioning in this discussion comparing the old model to the new is that in the old days you had to be available during the daytime. You had to be available for auditions; you had to be available to go into your agent's office; you had to be available to go into a recording studio. Meaning, you might have to take a night job to support yourself while building your voice over career.

Today it's a completely different game. The old model is outdated, it's dead, or at the very least it's taking a last breath. The old model barely has a pulse, and unfortunately your voice over business will barely have a pulse if you choose to wait for agents to call you for auditions.

If people tell you, "Hey, I'm going to get you into the voice over business.", ask them about their business plans. Better yet, ask to SEE a business plan. If they say it's all about being a great performer and having excellent vocal technique ... well, you know where I'm going here. That is not a business plan at all. It is a perfect recipe for failure.

Now, don't get me wrong, you have to be good. You need to learn technique and you absolutely have to be competitive. But those two qualities alone won't get you much of anything. The bottom line is that you absolutely must be willing and able to market yourself.

What I am telling you, and I'm telling you again to make a point, is that I'll make $250,000 this year strictly with my voice over work. For the past seven months I've averaged close to $5,000 each week. By my calculations that will result in $250,000 on an annual basis. This income figure is sustainable and it is growing. That's the exciting thing about it.

Now, the other side of that same coin is the fact that I am one person, and I only have so many hours in a day. This is the same issue any professional voice over person will face sooner or later. I only have so much physical ability, so much stamina. My income will eventually become limited by the number of hours in the day.

The same thing will be true for you, but your potential earnings can easily exceed $50,000 per year, believe me. Your ability to earn will be limited only by your ability to market yourself until you run out of hours in the day. Here's what I am saying - if I stopped working at noon every day for the next year, I'd make more than $50,000. There is plenty of voice over work out there.

And you can find voice over work wherever you live. In the past, in the old model, if you wanted to get jobs you had to live on the coast. You had to live in Los Angeles or New York. Maybe you could build a voice over career if you were a big player in your local market, in a decent sized market, such as Dallas or Philadelphia. But your career would not grow past the size of your local market.

For example, I came up through the ranks in Columbus, Ohio. That's where I worked in radio. I remember there were a few voices you would hear all the time on the radio in that area. They were full-time voice talent, but they were big fish in a relatively small pond.

One day about 25 years ago a gentleman came through the door of the radio station in Columbus and somebody looked at me and said, "That's so-'n-so. He makes $50,000 a year." He was one of the big voices in town and I'd heard him, but I had never seen him. That was back in the late 80s, and $50,000 a year sounded like a lot of money to me at the time.

But you can easily make that much now if you are willing to market yourself. And you can do it anywhere. You don't have to live in Los Angeles or New York, and you don't have to show up for an audition and sit in a waiting room with a couple dozen other people waiting to audition as well. You can audition from your home recording studio anytime.

Years ago when I was seriously considering building a career in voice over, I remember asking myself, "Am I willing to give up what I'm doing now to drive to auditions and sit there and wait around?" And I couldn't do it. I couldn't get motivated in the old model.

If things hadn't changed when the internet came along, I'd still be working at a radio station. Maybe I'd still be a college professor, or perhaps I'd be holding down a corporate job. But I would not be doing voice over, that's for sure.

Chapter 5

The New Voice Over Model - The Wave of The Future

Let me go more in-depth on what the new model looks like. It really boils down to the use of technology, and the availability of cheap technology that operates at a professional level. My first voice over studio was located in the master bedroom closet of my home. Fortunately, my wife was gracious enough to let me use some closet space, as long as it was on the side with my own clothes and not hers.

I invested about $300 in equipment, and that was all the money I had invested in my studio at the time. I am not suggesting you should start a career in voice over this way, but I was able to do it.

When I worked at the radio station I remember people saying you would have to invest at least $50,000 to have a serious voice over studio. But that was before computers, and all the necessary recording equipment represented a big investment. I didn't have all that money to invest in my new business.

Today I've got several thousand dollars in my studio, primarily in top quality microphones and digital editing software. I can send audio files instantly to my clients, and I can communicate online in order to market myself to production studios and businesses that need voice over talent.

The voice over business is cheap and fast now. It allows those of us who are not willing to work a job at night, so we can travel and audition for voice over jobs during the day, to build a business in the new model. It gave me a chance to build a business from my home, and it can do the same for you.

On the flip side of this new model is another new development. Because the business is cheap and fast now, everybody is suddenly a voice over talent. Or at least it seems that way. Tens of thousands of people participate on Voices.com, which is a huge voice casting website that serves the whole world.

Fortunately, the majority of voice talent on Voices.com are genuine, meaning they are properly trained in their profession of voice over. But – and this is the most significant point – most of them have no idea how to market themselves to get jobs. I had a conversation with a client who used that website to find talent, and he said he listened to at least 200 auditions before he hired me for his job.

More importantly, he said, "80% of what I hear on that site is not even a contender. I listen to two or three seconds and delete it." I say this as encouragement to everyone who is seriously pursuing voice over as a career. Yes, there is plenty of voice over competition. No, they don't know how to market themselves properly.

Most aspiring voice over talent is not adequately trained from a performance standpoint and they are definitely not trained from a business and marketing standpoint. But in the new model there are many more people in the game. That is one significant way the voice over business has changed.

Another significant way the voice over business has changed is that talent agents are still around, but only for the big jobs. We all want to do national television ads, and I get my fair share of them, but the only way to get those higher paying jobs is to work through an agent. I have had some great jobs I found online for national voice over work, but those jobs were the exception, not the rule.

A big company like Proctor and Gamble, one with a massive marketing budget and an in-house marketing agency, generally wants to deal with talent agents because it's easier. They would rather pay for the agent to deal with the voice over talent because they can budget for it. What they don't want is thousands of voice over talents contacting them directly.

Using an agent is a one-stop-shop for big clients. Using an agent also means that agent has vetted the talent. Corporations can trust the agent to sift out the voices that don't qualify for their high level jobs.

But if Proctor and Gamble posted an ad on craigslist they might get a thousand responses, and 99.9 % wouldn't even come close to qualifying for their job. Big clients know talent working with agents are more likely to be serious contenders.

You should also know there are growing opportunities for women in the voice over field. Although I've tried to get statistics on this, there are none available. But I can tell you from personal observation and my long involvement in the industry there are more and more women's voices on radio and television.

Female voices are becoming more prominent in general, but especially with the new in-store advertorials, which are clever, chatty explanations of product features and benefits.

As a man, I've often thought it would be so much easier for me to get jobs if I were a woman because there were fewer women involved in the industry, and that means less competition. On the other hand, I've had women tell me, "Bill, if I wasn't a woman... I just know there would be more work out there for me." In the end I think it all evens out.

There are plenty of successful women, and probably as many women as men, in this career now. If you are female, I think this is a great profession for you to consider. If you are a good communicator and you are willing to learn voice over technique along with marketing and business strategies, this career is perfect for you.

I don't think the influx of people into the voice over industry will slow down any time soon. It seems like an avalanche of people right now. Based on the number of people who contact me online and email me to ask questions, I can tell you a career in voice over appeals to many, many people. I could make a full-time job out of answering emails, if somebody would pay me to answer them.

It seems like everybody knows somebody who has an interest in being a voice over talent. When I meet new people and answer the typical question, "So, what do you do?", I often hear people say they would like to get into the field, or they know somebody else who is interested. I had no idea, until I got into the business, there were so many aspiring voice over talents on the planet.

Once again, all this competition is not a signal for you to back off. It is just the opposite. Lots of competition signals a healthy and growing industry, and it creates an environment where the fit will survive. You will become fit by understanding you can no longer be a successful voice over talent without also being a successful marketer.

Chapter 6

What It Takes To Be Successful –
Your Voice Over Career Path

Basically, you need a specific skill set to be successful voice over talent now. You must be able to read aloud, and even though you may be smiling as you read this, it is the rock-bottom reality of the voice over business. Voice over work is reading and speaking out loud. Some people simply cannot do that.

Some people really struggle when they attempt to read aloud, and to do so without stumbling or stammering. Reading aloud is a problem for many school children, and it is still a problem for many adults. If you have this problem, you need to be coached so you will improve. If you are a good reader and you simply have trouble reading aloud, you can usually overcome the problem.

Voice over talent read aloud all day long; we read aloud into a microphone, and sometimes we are required to read aloud in front of other people, such as production directors and marketing agency people. We have to be able to read aloud, and we have to be able to read aloud in front of an audience if necessary.

Voice over talent also need to be able to communicate, just as I mentioned at the very beginning of this book. Communicating means connecting with others and helping them understand a message. It means getting people to understand the message and to act on what they hear. This is a very important point.

Voice over talent use their voices to motivate people. Clients hire voice over talent for their skill in motivating other people, not just for the sound of their voices. We are salespeople, too. We are not simply performers. In commercials, in e-learning and in training we are selling concepts; we are trying to get people to do things and take action with what we say.

Essentially, we have the responsibility to get people to buy into what we are saying, so being a good communicator is critical.

If you are a good storyteller, you will be a good communicator. Remember, that's what we are doing - telling stories.

We are telling stories to motivate, persuade and inform people. Now you know why I like working with salespeople and pastors and teachers. They are already trained to motivate, persuade and inform other people.

You can see why I keep going back to communicating and to being a storyteller. If you can read out loud and communicate, you have the basic skills that are required to do voice over work. There is honestly nothing much needed beyond those skills. I mean, there's some technique involved, but if you can do those two things, chances are excellent that you can succeed in a voice over career.

By now you may be asking, "What will I have to read to do voice overs? Where does it come from, and how do I get it?" A script is what you read. The client gives you the script, already written. Your job is to read the script aloud and communicate the message clearly.

In order to read a script skillfully, you have to dissect it when you get it. Later in this book I will describe how to do that, but for now I'll simply say that you need to be able to look at a script and answer some basic questions: 1) Who is in the audience? 2) Who am I? 3) What is my role in this project? 4) What are we trying to accomplish?

Perhaps these questions will jump start your thinking process about dissecting and analyzing a script. You will be tearing the script apart in order to know it well, to own it, to master it. Owning the script means having confidence when you read it aloud. That confidence comes through in your voice. That confidence is what sets you apart from other voice over talent.

Your confidence comes through in the details as well. When you know how to tear a script apart to determine where to place emphasis, where to pause for effect, and where to exhibit emotion, you become a master of the script. You own it. And you own it without even thinking about these things while you are reading it aloud.

When I understand my role in the voice over production, and what the client has hired me to accomplish, I understand I am not just speaking words. I am communicating a message. Success in communicating comes from confidence and skill. I have confidence and skill now, but I didn't always have them, not at first.

How do you get confidence? You get confidence in voice over by reading scripts aloud, lots of scripts. I'll be honest with you, when I started this career I didn't have a great deal of confidence. I had a lot of desire, and I had some basic skills, but that's it. My skills needed to be improved, but my desire was enough to pull me through the learning curve to succeed.

Having the desire, I persevered with the work until I gained the confidence. If you have enough desire to succeed it will carry you through, too. Your desire will lead you to the place where you can get the confidence, the place where you develop a little swagger in what you do. When I say swagger I don't mean you get cocky, I mean you know you can do the job. Swagger is confidence.

Here's a picture of confidence for you, a story about my recent trip to the Wrigley Building in Chicago where I showed up at a big recording studio for a voice over job. Most of my work is done in my own home studio, but in the past couple of years I've gone out of my studio a couple times for big jobs. One of those jobs was a national radio commercial, and I had to travel to the studio in downtown Chicago.

As I went in to do the session, I was surprised to see six people from an advertising agency walk in the door after I arrived. I had to sit there and read the script aloud while taking direction from six different people. Does that sound like a nightmare? Strangely enough, I love that sort of challenge now.

But seven years ago I would have been overwhelmed. I would have been very self-conscious sitting there behind a pane of glass, unable to hear what was going on outside the sound booth. All I knew was that they were listening to me and they were watching me and taking notes.

I saw pencils and pens scribbling furiously, and then I saw them talking amongst themselves, but of course I couldn't hear them at all. I really wanted to get out of there, but of course I couldn't escape. Now I welcome this situation and no longer desire to escape.

If you can get to the place where you actually enjoy the scenario I just described, you will know you are ready for big time voice over work. You will know you can deliver what clients want because you have confidence in yourself. You will definitely experience a big thrill when you give clients what they want, and that's when you realize you can succeed. You know it because you begin to see your voice over success in action.

The reality of success is only reached by passing through the barren wasteland of fear, however. It's true. It was true for me and it will be true for you. Anxiety and apprehension are natural to this process. Everybody experiences them. The question is not, "Do you have fear?", because fear is inevitable. You cannot completely escape fear. The question is this – "Do you have enough desire to carry you through the fear to in order reach genuine confidence?" That is the real question.

While you are asking yourself that second question, consider another aspect of it. Knowing what you CAN do well and what you CAN'T do well is what enables you to succeed. It is the next step in the process fueled by your intense desire to succeed.

Knowing what you can do well will automatically cause a big breakthrough. Unfortunately, most of us come into voice over work with an idea in our mind. However, that idea may be all wrong.

We usually think we're supposed to sound a certain way, so most of us start out doing an impersonation of how we think we're supposed to sound. In other words, we miss the mark because we don't sound natural at all.

I hope this is making sense because it is really, really important. The idea that is stuck in our heads, the impression of what we think we should sound like, may actually be our worst problem.

We may get this idea from listening to other people on radio and television, and we may not even know we are unconsciously imitating them. Trying to sound like somebody else is futile, because that job is already filled. That job description is somebody else's, it is not yours.

You have to become very good at being yourself. Surprisingly, relaxing into the reality that you just need to be yourself when you are reading a script aloud may be your greatest challenge. Performers must have confidence and belief in themselves to bring something unique and different into their voice work. Even as a full-time voice over talent making really good money I continue to evolve and to gain confidence in different aspects of my performance.

Here is a tremendous clue for you. The first step to knowing what you can do well is knowing what you can't do well. Yes, it is ok to admit that there are things you can't do well. Let me be the first to admit there are certainly voice over jobs I cannot do well. That's right. There are high paying jobs I would love to do, but I am simply not the man for the job.

Let me start by telling you what I choose to avoid in order to invest my time making money. I recently completed a movie trailer for Madagascar 3, not for the major cinematic release that came out last year, but for the current on-demand version of the film.

While I don't usually do movie trailers, the on-demand release trailer format worked for me. My sound is not a block-buster, action-packed movie trailer sound. I am not a four-wheel-drive truck commercial guy, a big rugged masculine voice – that's not my expertise. I avoid those jobs.

I avoid certain jobs in order to focus on the jobs I can do well. That is how I satisfy my clients and build my six figure voice over business. And let me share one more example of something I choose to avoid now. It is funny because I was still learning what I am telling you now, and this incident occurred before under-stood it.

I was contacted by a gentleman in Las Vegas who was looking for a ring announcer. I'd actually done a commercial for this guy in the past, and he was also involved with professional boxing in Las Vegas. He asked me to audition for the job of ring announcer because he wanted to shoot a video. So, I thought maybe I could pull it off. I recorded my best impersonation of a ring announcer and sent him a demo.

I never heard back from the guy, and I honestly think it was because my demo was terrible. I'm just not cut out for the loud, in-your-face, obnoxious, boxing ring announcer thing. I'm more laid back. Announcing a boxing match is not consistent with my nature. It's just not me. Pretending to be a boxing ring announcer was an excellent learning experience. It taught me a great lesson on the subject of knowing what I can do well and what I can't do well.

You will have your own lessons, too. It is an important part of the process of discovering who you are. Your best voice over work is not too far removed from who you are as a person. It's really about learning to be yourself and learning to market your-self. I am best suited to presenting information. That is who I am as a person, a learner and a teacher. I do a lot of e-learning work because I am highly in demand for it and I have the right sound for it.

You will also learn who you are, and what you should do, by the jobs you get. You will naturally begin to understand what you can do well because people will start asking you to do more and more of it. That just makes sense, doesn't it? You will be offered more jobs you can do well and less jobs you can't do well. It's a natural process that just takes time to unfold.

Hitting that sweet spot, the center, the core of YOU is what I call the Money Voice. I know my own Money Voice, and when I coach people I help them find their personal Money Voice. I don't mean to say that's all you will ever do, but it will be the goal.

The closer you get to jobs that require your personal Money Voice, the more money you will earn. Think of it as a target; your Money Voice is the bull's eye in the center of the target. It's your dead center. My Money Voice is who I am at my most comfortable, at my best.

Once you make your way to finding your Money Voice, you can begin to explore some areas around it. You begin to discover what else you can do. When I coach people my first goal is to help them identify their Money Voice, and my second goal is to help them explore the area immediately surrounding it. Chances are good there are some things you can do that you don't even recognize yet. But you can find them with a little pushing and prodding from me.

For instance, I produce demo recordings for some of my clients, and we go through that process in a very intense manner. I give them a lot of different scripts and I have them read the scripts aloud. As I listen, I'm trying to figure out exactly what people can do well, and what they can't do well. And I may encourage them to stretch in areas where they excel, and avoid areas where they are merely average. The goal is to cultivate their talent to compete in the marketplace.

Remember, there are countless people who are talented. There are huge websites full of professional voice over talent demos and performers waiting to be hired. But, the reality of the voice over business is that there are not that many people who make a great living doing voice over work, and it is simply because they lack the business and marketing know-how. They only have half of the necessary equation for success.

What I keep telling you was actually a great revelation for me at one point. Understanding that the business and marketing aspect is half the equation of voice over success took me by surprise, believe it or not.

Even with my business background I had the wrong idea, just as many other people have the wrong idea. I just assumed voice over was a completely different animal, that no rules applied, and that nothing else I'd ever done in business would apply here. But, I was totally wrong; everything I had learned in business applied to my voice over business.

Business is business is business, and if you understand some basic business and marketing principles you will be miles ahead of your competition. Start thinking now: Who is in my audience? How do I get in front of those people? How do I get them to remember me? How do I serve them so they want me to speak again and again and again? This inquiry is not complicated at all. It is a lot of concentrated mental work, but it is not difficult.

I've worked very, very hard, but it's not complicated work. I basically just do the same thing every day, over and over again. It is simple, but it is not easy.

Here's what I mean – it is simple because there are only a few things you need to master. It is not like becoming a surgeon. You don't have to go to college for 12 years and learn human anatomy and how medicines affect it. But it's not easy because most people don't have the tenacity to persevere and to succeed.

Truthfully, it took about 100 auditions for me to land my first job on one of the big websites I mentioned previously. I experienced what Seth Godin calls The Dip, and the phenomenon he describes in his book with the same title.

It's an interesting and entertaining book. You should take the time to read it because it explains how we generally have to work like a crazy person for a long time to gain the skill and the confidence to get to the other side. Everybody has to persevere to get through The Dip.

I persevered by submitting about 100 auditions before I got my first job. You may find yourself persevering, too. Perseverance has nothing to do with talent. Even the very talented among us must learn to persevere. When I am coaching people I make sure they understand this important concept and somewhat harsh reality, and I am prepared to remind them over and over if necessary.

I just got an email from one of my students this week. He asked me if I remembered him calling me when he had submitted 100 auditions, and again when he had submitted 150 auditions. I kept telling him, "Great! You are doing it right!" To make a long story short, now he is doing really well because he didn't quit. He made it through The Dip and he came out the other side. He is successful in his voice over career now.

Let me be sure to provide a caveat here, a warning in fact. If you are doing the wrong thing and you don't quit doing it, that is not going to lead you to success. You cannot persevere doing the wrong thing and succeed.

Honestly, but that is just stupid. Ignorance and stupidity are two totally different things. A person can be ignorant and willing to learn, willing to change, but a person can also refuse to learn and change. Refusing to learn and change is what I consider stupid.

My point here is that having the right plan and following it will lead you to success if you persevere. Success won't happen on the first day, but it will happen eventually.

It took me 100 auditions to get my first job, but once got it, I gained more confidence and knew I must be onto something. I learned to market myself better and that boosted my confidence even more. From that point it was an upward spiral to more and more success. This spiral is built on three basic qualities. I developed these qualities and you can develop them, too.

These three basic qualities in the upward spiral of success are focus, persistence, and tenacity. Focus means single-mindedness. You have to approach your voice over work as a successful business in the making, from the very start. You can't think of it as messing around behind a microphone just to see what happens.

If you proceed on an experimental basis you probably won't make it in this business. Building a six figure voice over business requires a massive amount of effort on the front end, over an extended period of time. You can do it on a part-time basis, yes, but be prepared to give it a great deal of time and tremendous effort in the beginning.

You have to treat your business very seriously, you have to focus, and then your persistence and tenacity will kick in. Persistence and tenacity are two of the most highly paid attributes anyone can develop. If you are willing to keep going back into the fray over and over again, if you are willing to get back on that horse and ride, you will eventually succeed. That's just how it works.

Here's another warning: as performers, we tend to take everything personally. If we don't get a job, we think we must be terrible. And, maybe we are terrible, but that is unlikely. I was a terrible boxing announcer, for sure. But that doesn't mean I was a terrible voice over talent. I just wasn't the man for that particular job. There were other people auditioning for the boxing ring announcer job and some of them were more suited for it than I was.

The silence after my boxing ring announcer demo submission helped me learn I must have extremely sharp focus on what I do well. I have to be the right person for a job in order to accomplish it and to succeed. My voice over career has been, and continues to be, a succession of jobs I do well. I look for them, I find them, I fulfill them, and that is how I build my success.

When there are 200 other people auditioning for the job you want it is pretty silly to take rejection personally. They are probably all pretty good, and somebody may be better than you for the job. If you are willing to hang in there long enough the right doors will open for you. You will get an opportunity to be very good at being yourself and your demo will outshine the rest. You will get the job because you are the right person for the job. It will be obvious to the client, and it will be obvious to you.

Chapter 7

Union vs. Non-Union Voice Over Jobs

I must admit something up front about this chapter -- it is not my favorite subject. I'm not an expert on union affairs when it comes to voice over work. I look at everything with a birds-eye view, however, and I can share the observations and conclusions I've reached over the years.

First of all, the two big organizations are SAG and AFTRA, the Screen Actor's Guild and the American Federation of Television and Radio Artists. In fact, these two organizations have recently combined.

It's interesting, because just as talent agents have lost power over time, unions are losing their power, too. In the face of this loss of power SAG and AFTRA decided to combine forces to survive.

I know that both unions have worked hard to provide for actors and voice over talent and other people involved in media. They have bargained for benefits actors and other members did not have in the past, such as retirement and medical benefits.

There are certain requirements for membership in the union, but I'm not an expert on that at all. I could not give you the specifics on membership qualification, but I would urge you to contact the SAG and AFTRA offices to get all the current information available.

I am a non-union voice talent. If I were to accept work during a union strike I would be called a scab. There have been strikes in the past and that is what non-union talent were called when they stepped in to take union jobs during the strike. That was before I started doing voice over work, however, so it is not part of my experience.

If you are a member of the union, you can only accept jobs that are union jobs. I have always felt that limiting myself to union jobs would limit my possibilities and restrict what I could do. I know I can get a lot of work because I am a good marketer. And I firmly believe that if I belonged to the union I would be earning far less money than I earn today.

Now, that being said, I need to admit that almost all the seven figure voice talent now are union members. They have been able to compete at the highest levels, and they are consistently offered the best jobs. There are very few of them, though.

Most union talent, from my understanding, averages about $4,000 a year income from union voice over jobs. Voice over is a part-time occupation for them, and I understand there are fewer and fewer opportunities for union voice over work available in the marketplace.

Being non-union, I can work with anybody on any project I choose. I don't have to worry about it, and even if I don't get paid as much per job, or get residuals or royalties, I make an excellent income.

Unions negotiate on behalf of their members, but I negotiate for myself. I like it that way because I do a good job negotiating as well as producing the voice over work.

For instance, most of my jobs are buy-out work. When I record a television commercial I am paid "x" number of dollars, one time -- that is all I will receive from the job. I don't get paid every time the commercial airs, as I would get paid as a union member.

I can hear some of you thinking and wondering right now... why I choose not to be a member of the union. I will tell you plainly I choose to be non-union talent because there aren't as many opportunities for union members now. There are some great opportunities at the highest level, yes, but for the average voice over talent there is less and less work available now.

My advice to voice over talent who are just beginning a career is to start out non-union. That way you will get as much work as possible to build your income. It's much harder, from my experience and observation, to build your income when you start out as a union member. The jobs you get as a non-union member may not pay as well, but you are likely to get more jobs. It's that simple. You will earn more because you will get more work.

This is a good time to visit my website, which is www.Voice-Over-Training.org because it is the best way to get direct access to the latest information from me. I will keep you informed about the industry and send links to my free voice over tutorials.

I have created over 100 video tutorials on YouTube that are absolutely free. I record tutorials on an on-going basis, and I always email my people to let them know what I've posted.

Also, I share links to recent blog posts and announcements for events coming up, as well as my products and services available at special discounts. Link to me and you're linked to all things voice over. Sign up at Voice-Over-Training.org and you will be in my loop.

As a special bonus when you sign up, I'll give you a free 30-minute audio program called "Seven Steps to a Six Figure Voice Over Income". That program is basically a condensed version of this book, so you will want to listen to it and share it, too.

That audio program is a great tool to have on your iPod. It gives you a condensed version of what you are learning in order to build a successful voice over business and a successful career. I encourage you to sign up on my email list.

We all need new information and encouragement. I frequently search the web for relevant information, and I talk to my clients and my peers to bring you the news about what's happening in voice over. Since the audio link is a condensed version of this book, you will definitely appreciate hearing my main points over and over again.

Chapter 8

Why Being an Announcer Can Kill
Your Voice Over Career Before It Begins

In this chapter I need to go deeper into the subject of the dreaded announcer voice. No, I am not just talking about a boxing ring announcer. That is one classic type of announcer that would be included, of course, but I am referring to all types of announcers now.

Please hear me when I tell you there is a very strong prejudice against radio announcers in general. I had to overcome my radio announcer habits to build my voice over career.

Talent agencies and casting directors, on behalf of their corporate and creative clients, are looking for communicators, not announcers. An announcer is a voice "talking at" an audience, rather than "talking to" the audience. Announcers are up high somehow, and their audience is down low. This is a very subtle and yet very significant difference. None of us likes to feel talked down to, do we? Even children don't like it. Nobody likes it, it doesn't work well.

As a former radio announcer, I know exactly what not to do. Radio announcers have to squeeze 35 to 40 seconds of scriptwriting into a 30 second window of time. That is what I was paid to do all day long when I was a radio announcer. I did it for years, and now I have to avoid doing it all day long in order to succeed.

In most cases, radio announcers read scripts that were written by the owner of the business that purchased radio air time. Sometimes the business owners paid professional writers, but in Columbus, Ohio, where I worked as a radio announcer, budgets were tight. We all became proficient at speed reading on the air. The clients wanted to get their money's worth, so they figured the more words we could read, the better their commercial would work.

Cramming words into a short time slot as an announcer is the total opposite of what I do now as voice talent. Not always, but generally speaking, I get to read well-written copy that allows for normal breathing and dramatic pauses whenever appropriate. Scripts are written by professionals and the result is completely the opposite of those harried radio commercials I had to read in the past. I am thankful for that because I excel at a natural, normal reading pace now.

But radio people who break into voice over often struggle with this issue. Announcers are too familiar with the process of speeding through a script, so they seem to balk at the notion of taking their time to read naturally. Voice over work is a completely different paradigm. It is not announcing, it is communicating. You might think this is merely a mindset, but it is actually a skill set as well.

Folks, I am not making this up. I'm explaining this in detail for those of you who come from a radio background, as well as those who have listened to radio announcers and may be imitating them. Do not assume anything you know about announcing, or anything you can do or anything you have learned about it, will work in the voice over business. It will not work now. It will backfire badly.

Honestly, you will probably have to reconstruct yourself, just as I did. Most of the scripts I receive for commercials actually say, in writing, "No radio announcer." Either the client or the agent has made it clear that the voice over talent holding that script is on notice that the sound of an announcer is not wanted.

I cannot tell you the number of times I have seen the words, "No radio announcer" written on a script. And I've worked recording sessions during which I've been stopped as I was reading the script. This is embarrassing, but I heard words like these more than once, "Hey, stop sounding like a radio announcer. Cut it out. Cut it out now!" Oh boy, that was not good. My announcer voice had become so engrained over the years I had to work hard to overcome it. I really struggled to subdue it.

Here is how you can tell the difference, now and in the future. Remember what I learned and maybe you won't have to hear words like that when you are recording. I learned that if I am a radio announcer I am really not listening to the words as much as I'm listening to the sound of my own voice. I am acting, I am not communicating.

Let's let that point sink in for a moment. If you have been involved in radio work, or if you have listened to a lot of radio over the years, you will have to give this issue some serious consideration. An announcer is not communicating; that person is acting. Clients today want to hire communicators, not actors.

To highlight the difference, consider what I am doing right now. I am writing, but I am using a conversational, readable style. I am not barking commands at you. If you are in announcer mode in your career, or even in your fantasies, you have to stop in order to succeed in voice over work. Sounding like an announcer will not get you jobs or build your career; not now, not ever.

Radio announcers are on automatic pilot. They are trained and they respond to their training with great efficiency and skill. Basically, they are in a rut. Announcers do things automatically, and they keep doing them over and over. Give me a script for a car dealership, or a local pet store or a maid service. It doesn't matter, I'm going to read them all the same if I am an announcer.

I am going to read fast, without much variation. I just have to get the words out and get the job done. Are you getting my drift here? I hope so, because I am describing what you can never do if you want to survive the initial stages of your voice over career. Almost like an addict, you have to kick your habit. You have to break the habit of slipping into your announcer voice, and you have to keep it in check forever.

So, how do you break the announcer habit? You have to take

it upon yourself to shake yourself up, slap your own face, and get into a completely different frame of mind. I hate to admit it, but sometimes I will yell, or scream, or start reading in a cartoon voice. I still have to do that, even now, whenever I hear myself slipping into the dreaded announcer voice I used for so many years in radio.

I will choose a character, maybe a pirate, and I will slip into a pirate voice for a few minutes, just to break out of my old, habitual rut. It has to be completely outrageous in order to slap me silly. Then, in a few minutes, I find that I can read naturally again. By the way, I did not create this technique. Actors have used this method for many years, mostly because it works.

Sometimes you have to just get completely out of your current state of mind, your rut, in order to break free and do your job. It is amazing to me how well this technique works for me. If I voice the first 10 seconds of a commercial like a pirate, which would be totally ridiculous for this commercial, and then I stop, when I go back and start from the top it's amazing how much more relaxed I become. Somehow I am freed to become myself.

In case this particular technique doesn't work for you, feel free to get someone to smack you in the face, or to do whatever it takes to shake you loose and jar you out of the announcer rut. Better a smack in the face than a great career in voice over lost to an old, bad habit.

Chapter 9

Voice Over Performance Skills

I hope nothing I have shared so far in this book has led you to the conclusion that if you excel in marketing yourself you will not need voice over performance skills. That would be wrong, and I would have led you astray.

What you need is a specific skill set; you don't need a world-class speaking voice to make money as a voice over artist. However, you do need to be good at what you do well. You need to apply a skill set to exactly who you are, and then you will develop the confidence and the reputation that will help you get jobs and build a career.

It all goes back to the concept of storytelling. If you are intimidated by a script, just remember you are merely telling a story. We have all read stories that were easy to read, and we have read others that were difficult. The quality of script writing for voice over work is usually quite high, which means it is easier to read.

Radio scripts are usually much harder to read because the quality of the writing is lower. I think radio people often suffer when they make the transition to better scripts simply because they are not familiar with the writing.

What is going on in my head when I pick up a script to analyze it is probably more complicated than I can adequately describe. I'll do my best to share my thoughts with you now, so bear with me as I work through them.

Unlike an announcer who has to be a speed reader and cram too many words into a short time slot, a voice over talent has to be more of an interpreter and a guide through the script. I have to make the message easy to understand as I read the script aloud. It's not just the words I read, but how I read them that conveys the message clearly.

When I'm telling a story (reading a script) I have to be aware of many things at one time. I do this automatically now, but I've had a lot of practice. I ask my questions, you know, the four questions I mentioned earlier: 1) Who is in the audience? 2) Who am I? 3) What is my role in this project? 4) What are we trying to accomplish? And then I ask some more questions, too.

For instance, will I be talking as a detached third person, narrating what's going on? Am I playing the part of somebody giving a testimonial? Am I involved in the action, or am I describing the actions going on? So, who am I and what's my role? The other thing is, who am I talking to? Who is my audience?

If I'm talking to a youngster I will speak in a different tone than I would use talking to a senior citizen. If you don't understand who you're talking to, you cannot communicate well. Think of it in terms of real life - whenever you're talking to your child you may speak differently than talking to your parent or grandparent.

It may seem that an age difference is not so important, but it is actually the relationship difference that matters. We all speak in a different tone or manner to a spouse, a boss, a co-worker, a pastor, a judge, or a stranger. Start listening to how you speak to others and you will see what I mean.

In a television commercial I saw for a minivan, a mother was driving her child, who was strapped into a car seat in the back. The mother was speaking, but her mouth was not moving. The voice over was actually the thoughts in her mind while she was driving. She was describing the safety features of the minivan, but she was speaking in a whisper because the baby was asleep in the back seat. The voice talent honored the context of the script by whispering the script, so as not to wake the baby. To me, this commercial exemplifies the idea of, "where we are in the script."

You also want to consider what you are trying to accomplish

as you read the script. What does the client want to happen? Are they selling something? Are they providing information? Do they need you to elicit emotion in the audience? Do they need you to move people to action? Do they want the audience to get excited so they will be motivated to go to see the latest movie or buy the latest product? Are you trying to instill a sense of confidence in a brand of products?

Many emotions and goals may be determined by asking questions like these. And, of course, there could be a whole range of emotions and goals for any one project. You will get in touch with those goals and emotions by studying scripts, and over time you will begin to get a feel for the right questions and the right answers to ask in order to know how the script should be handled.

This seems like a good time to share something I call the Three Swing Technique, a name I stole from the golf channel. A golf instructor was talking about a Three Swing Technique he uses to teach his students. It means you take two practice swings with the golf club so that by the third swing you are ready to hit. You take the practice swings to get the feel of the shot.

And as I watched the instructor, I was thinking how his golf technique reminds me of the way I read a script. I basically take three swings with it. I do a first read through just to get a sense of who I am as the reader, who am I talking to as the audience, what words I will be using to communicate, and what special things I need to notice in the script. I pay attention to these details the first time around so they become easy and natural for me.

The second time I go through the script, I record it as if it's for real, but I know it's not; it's really a practice run-through. And then I go back and listen to the practice recording, attempting to hear it as the audience will hear it.

Normally, on the third swing, or read-through, or maybe the

fourth time if necessary, it's a pretty good read. I take the time to find the groove and get the sense of what the script is saying so I know how to read it in order to convey the message well. That's a short description of my Three Swing Technique.

To be really sure I get a good final read on the script, I like to mark it up. I go through it and identify parts of the script that may be more important than other, or places that might benefit from a pause or a change in voice inflection. I am making the script my own at this point, and that is how I come to own it, to manage it, and to succeed in reading it well.

I go back and look for key words and phrases. This is so obvious it might sound funny, but the most important word or phrase in a script is always the name of the business or product being advertised or promoted. That's always the most important, so you have to make sure it stands out. Quite simply, the client won't be happy unless they hear the name emphasized. No matter what follows the name, it will not count if the name is not clearly heard and understood.

In a 30-second script, every microsecond counts. Every word, every phrase, every nuance counts, so I underline or highlight the key benefits and descriptions in order to read them and convey the message well. My audience must be able to get the point, whether it's something exciting, something new, something that's a great value, or whatever the case may be.

When I talk about underlining and highlighting, I want to be clear about what I mean. Some people use pens and highlighters on hard copies of scripts. I used to do that, too. But now I work in Word documents and PDFs on my computer screen. I use the underlining and highlighting functions in Word to mark up my scripts.

Surprisingly, I have learned to use a font size that is as small as I can read and still be able to see it clearly. The reason for this choice is quite simple. The less my eyes have to scan back and forth, the fewer mistakes I make, especially in long form narration. Most people think that larger fonts would be easier to read, and I thought that, too, for many years. But one day I just stumbled on the idea of a using small, compact font.

In fact, I had been thinking I was making too many mistakes and wondering how could I remedy the problem. Suddenly I realized my head was moving back and forth a lot because I was scanning long scripts from side to side. I could see the words really well, but I couldn't get the best sense of each sentence or every paragraph. When I tried shrinking the script down to 10- or 11-point fonts, I could really see it all, I could get the big picture. As a result my mistakes dramatically decreased.

As regards marking up a script, you are doing whatever needs to be done to enhance your most important performance tool, which is your voice. You need to be conscious of the fact that your voice is your performance tool.

For one thing, if you are not recording, you are not making money. For another thing, if you don't sound quite right, if you are just feeling "off", no matter what you do it will come through in the recording. You just can't fake the sound of you at your best.

But going back, just to give you a few more things to keep in mind when you're marking up your script - start by highlighting key words, phrases, descriptions, adjectives and key benefits, and then you super-charge it all with the Money Line. That's the word or phrase or sentence that is the big punch line, the real payoff. If you can pick out the Money Line, you can give it special attention and cause it to stand out and rise above the rest of the script.

I don't mean you need a megaphone to get the point across. You certainly don't need to shout it or even speak louder (no announcers, remember?) but you give it special treatment. Identifying the Money Line in your demo can put you 'way above' anybody else who's competing for a job.

Let me give you a perfect example. Tim Allen recently recorded a Chevy Cruze commercial. If you go to YouTube and type in Chevy Cruze Tim Allen New Kid you will find the commercial. New Kid is the name of the commercial.

To me, Tim Allen is the master of the guy next door. He has a very unassuming manner about him. He doesn't have a really big voice of God; he has the voice of an average guy, maybe your next door neighbor. He sounds very ordinary, but he thoroughly understands the context of a script. In fact, I've never seen anybody better at interpreting a script than Tim Allen.

This commercial compares the Chevy Cruze to other vehicles. It mentions the quietness, and goes on to say that Autoblog says it is as quiet as a Lexus. And then right before the tag line, which is the last sentence, Tim Allen says, "So much for the new kid fitting in with the rest of the class."

That is the Money Line because it is the transition point. It is the hinge the tag line hangs on and it fastens the first part of the script to the last part of the script. It has to be there or everything falls apart. The Money Line is where everything turns to money. It leads the audience from features and benefits to the very last line of the script.

When Tim Allen pauses, you can actually hear a little smile in his voice. His Money Line is different from the rest of the script and you know he is raising his eyebrow when he says, "So much for the new kid fitting in with the rest of the class." Tim Allen nails it right there.

When you get a sense of the Money Line in your script, and you remember you are not a radio announcer who reads straight through it as fast as possible, that's when you arrive. Knowing and owning the Money Line is what separates the pros from the wanna-be pros. Finding the Money Line and giving it special treatment is the key to your professional success in voice over.

It may be a pause, a slower pace, or it may be a facial expression you use while you read, such as a smile, a wink, or a nod. Those things influence the sound of your voice and the audience can actually hear them. Check out Tim Allen's YouTube video, and you will hear exactly what I am saying. Then start practicing it yourself; you can do it, too.

These are the subtle things that win auditions and get jobs. Never forget the Money Line and your clients will never forget you. You will soon be 'way down the road' towards building your six figure voice over business.

Before we move on to a discussion of various types of scripts, I need to talk about what to do when you're having some vocal problems or feeling under the weather. As I said, how you feel will definitely show up in your voice work. When you are a full-time voice over talent and you're feeling bad, or if your voice has got some problems, you are simply not at the top of your game. That is not good.

Let's say you wake up and you are a little hoarse or stuffed up. Those things are not conducive to great voice over perform-ance. I always try to remember the best offense is a good defense. Obviously, taking care of yourself is important. Avoiding a cold can save you a lot of hassle and lost work time. Just do the things your mom warned you about when you were young, such getting plenty of sleep and protecting yourself from windy, wet and cold weather.

As simple as that sounds, it's really huge. Get plenty of sleep and be sure to stay hydrated; always drink plenty of water. That alone can help you avoid problems with congestion. Personally, I'm prone to allergies at certain times of the year but I respond well to Claritin, so I keep a supply on hand and take it every day. I'm thankful to have a good relationship with my family doctor who prescribes antibiotics, too, if necessary.

For heaven's sake, if you feel the symptoms of a sinus infec-tion, get to your doctor. I have those crop up at least once a year, and I take care of them immediately because I cannot afford to lose my voice. The point is, pay attention to your health and treat yourself as you would care for your child. You have to think ahead in order to preserve your voice.

I also use a Neti Pot, available at drug stores. It is small and made of plastic, but it is shaped like a teapot. You put warm water in it along with a saline solution that's included with the pot. It is shaped so that you can easily pour the saline liquid in one nostril, allowing it to run back into your sinuses and then exit out your other nostril. I admit, that may sound a bit nasty, but it has a very satisfying and cleansing effect.

Some singers, actors and voice over talent swear that avoiding dairy products is a secret to good respiratory health. Personally, I wouldn't be so quick to say never use dairy products. What I have learned over time is that some of the conventional wisdom does not necessarily work for everyone.

For example, I've heard that eating green apples will reduce mouth noise. But it actually produces terrible mouth noise for me. That particular suggestion doesn't work for me.

The best thing for me is chewing gum. I frequently chew gum between recording sessions. It serves to cleanse everything and it is also a great reducer of mouth noise for me. Extra spearmint is my weapon of choice.

Going back to dairy products and the subject of avoiding them to reduce mucus in your system, if you are drinking a lot of milk you will probably have a mucus problem eventually. However, sometimes I use milk strategically as a tool. I drink it on purpose to change my voice. I do a lot of long form narration, so it's not uncommon for me to record hours of audio in one day, working on a project nonstop.

I do take short breaks periodically, but it's very stressful. And it physically hurts. So sometimes I'll just take a small cup of milk in the studio and I'll take sips, not big gulps, just little sips throughout the session. Sipping milk that way provides a coating on my throat and gives me enough relief to keep going and push through. I usually drink 2% milk when I do this. I also keep throat lozenges handy.

I've also heard many people suggest that it's good to refrain from drinking coffee. But I drink coffee all morning until lunch time. I've been drinking it that way for the last couple of decades, so I guess maybe I'm acclimated to it.

Hot tea, on the other hand, creates mouth noise for me. Coffee doesn't. The hot coffee loosens everything up, and until I've had a cup or two I'm not at my best. I can tell a huge difference after I've had one or two cups of coffee.

To complete this chapter on performance skills, we need to consider scripts, the differences in various types of scripts and how to deal with them. I'll tell you how I deal with them to build my successful voice over business.

With experience, you will begin to understand how commercial scripts can actually help you to interpret the words easier and read better. Commercial scripts are written by professional writers who have the expertise and the experience to think and plan ahead for the best performance by voice over talent. There are some basic rules to follow, but for our purposes in this book we don't need to go into them deeply. There will be plenty of time for that later.

One thing you will need to know to produce your first demo is that the first line of the script is the most important. Basically, the first line is the headline, and it's what grabs the attention of the listener and keeps, or loses, it. You have three or four seconds to grab the listener's attention. That's all. Keep that in mind as you begin reading any script.

When I use the word "grab", don't misunderstand my point. Grabbing, catching, snaring or nabbing all sound like hunting and trapping words. Maybe they don't sound good to you, but they sound great to your clients who are paying you to capture the attention of many listeners.

Capturing attention may require a big and exciting sound, or it may require something as soft as a whisper. The way you read the first line of a script should cause the listener to lean forward, closer to the speaker or the radio or the television. Picture that in your mind when you begin to read. That's a picture of the rapt attention your clients desire.

A commercial script usually includes a list of features and benefits which describe what the product will do and what it does for the person. Features describe the product and benefits describe what it does for you. Understand these, know the difference and practice giving them special treatment.

Make the features and benefits stand out when you read them. But always remember, you are not announcing them to an audience; you are sharing the information with a close friend. That is how you should read them, in most cases.

Also remember that underlining or highlighting a script to mark the places where you need to place emphasis when you are reading will help your performance. Give yourself every possible advantage, including several practice runs before your final take.

Every script is different, of course, but very often there will be a call to action toward the end of a script. That means you are encouraging, inviting or inspiring the listener to act. The call to action is often repeated because it may be a phone number, an address or a website. In order to take the next step, the listener has to remember where to go. Once again, you are not issuing an order like a drill sergeant. You want to sound like a trusted friend.

I've been in some recording sessions where I heard, "OK, let's go back and do the telephone numbers again because I need to make sure they hear those and they get those. So, let's slow it down and let's punch it a little bit."

The director is telling me to slow down, but give it a little more emphasis. This is a good example of real-life voice over work in a studio with directors, so you can see that reading and understanding the script beforehand will help you produce the best voice over work possible, under any circumstances.

Your best work is your best marketing tool. Never forget that. Your best work for every client, every time, not just the clients who pay the most. Taking the time to own and master the script, to honor it prior to recording it is the way you show respect for your clients and build your six figure voice over business for the long run.

All that being said, when I'm working in my home studio I prioritize my work for the best flow during each day. For instance, I may have a regional commercial to record that day, but I also have a couple of pages of training narration. Training narration is not nearly as demanding as commercial work where every nuance of every word, every phrase needs to be purposeful. Training narration is just natural talking, for the most part.

So I'll do a few pages of narration, maybe a training script or maybe an audio book first thing in the morning before I start the heavy, detail-oriented commercial work. Just reading a narration script loosens everything up for me. I get in the flow, in the groove. After that, I'm ready to rock and roll with more difficult scripts.

Chapter 10

Office Tools For
Professional Voice Over Talent

You are a professional, so you must be prepared to conduct business in a professional manner. I don't mean you will be required to have tools that are elaborate or extensive because I believe in simplicity. Less can definitely be more in the home recording studio. That's my approach.

There are some things every professional voice over talent needs in order to produce good work. At the very least, you absolutely must have reliable internet service because you will be marketing yourself, you will be communicating with your clients, and you will be sending your work via the internet almost every time.

Your internet service should be reliable and it should be reasonably fast. Remember that you will be uploading files that could be 50-100 megabytes or more in size, and you need to make sure it doesn't take three or four hours to accomplish an upload. So, rural satellite internet connections are not ideal, not at all. Dial-up internet connections don't work well either. You need DSL or cable with the best speeds your provider offers.

In case you are curious at this point, know that I will discuss ISDN later in this book. It's another subject for another chapter. If you don't know what ISDN is, relax. I will definitely explain it later.

Besides your internet connection, you will need a separate computer for your office and your studio functions. Your office computer doesn't have to be anything fancy, but it has to run a suite of Office programs such as Microsoft Word and Excel for basic documents. You need to be able to create and send invoices. Macintosh computers with Apple software will also work for your office.

For my accounting purposes I use Quicken Home and Office, not necessarily because it's better than anything else, but because it's just as good. It works for what I do and it's easy. Here's the thing - don't complicate your life. My suggestions are based on my choice to keep my life simple, and I'm encouraging you to do the same.

I keep all of my clients in a database. In my previous careers I've worked with some of top customer relationship management software (CRM), such as SalesForce and Act, but I avoid using them in my voiceover business. I use Outlook simply because it's easy and it works for me.

I want to keep track of my clients' names, their contact information, and all of my emails with them. That's really all I need. I mean, if you spend all your time managing a customer relationship management software program you have a lot less time for voice over work. I would rather work and earn money. That is my priority.

With regard to storage, I keep most of my finished voice work in the cloud. I keep copies of the work I do for each client and I store it in the cloud because I like redundancies. To prove my point, my house was recently struck by lightning and electricity fried a lot of my equipment. My recordings were safe in the cloud.

Was the good Lord angry with me for some unknown reason? I don't know. I can't answer that question, but I can certainly agree with the people who tell you to be prepared for this type of emergency situation. They, and now I always say "it's not if, but when..." Fortunately, my studio stayed in good shape, but I lost a lot of related gear. I was glad I had cloud backups in place.

You can't be too cautious when it comes to audio files. You don't want to lose audio files because you never know when you may need them again as reference for yourself, or because a client may ask for them. So I keep one set on an external hard drive, and I keep another set in the cloud. That way, even if I lose one I've still got the other.

I guess it's easy to see that when I say simple is better, I literally mean simple is better. I run a very lean, clean office so that I can devote my time and energy to the activities that generate income.

I only get paid when I'm marketing myself and when I'm recording. Everything else is support work. Obviously, some things are necessary to support the income-generating work, so I plan my life to have the most time available for recording voice overs that generate profit.

You might say that focus is the key to my six figure voice over business – I focus on voice over and marketing. I work IN my business as much as possible, and I work ON my business as little as possible.

That is not the same formula you may have heard from other business advisors, but I guarantee you that those people are not voice over talent. I am. And I am very successful as a voice over talent because I know what comes first and I do it every day.

Chapter 11

Your Six Figure Voice
Over Business Home Studio

Your home studio is where it all starts. It is the crucible, the womb, the birthplace of your six figure income. We have already discussed the old model versus the new model in previous chapters, but now is a good time to recall that the whole new model is based on the fact you can work from home now. That fact changed the voice over business completely, and it explains why everybody wants to do it now. It's relatively cheap, and it's easy. So your home studio is where it all begins.

In the past two years or so I've only worked outside my studio a couple times. Once I had a technical problem with my ISDN, which we'll talk about later, so I had to go downtown to record.

The other was my first job for a new audio book publisher, and they wanted to have me come into their studios to work with their engineers. It was the beginning of a relationship and they felt more comfortable with me being in their studio. Since then I've recorded four or five more books for them, all in my own studio.

Once you have your own studio there is very little you cannot do. Achieving a quiet space is the main thing. This is the basic struggle everybody faces. And we'll talk a little bit about gear, but you can have the best gear, the best equipment, and the best microphone, but if you've got a terrible space to record in, nothing else matters. You cannot put a price on a quiet space.

Let's say you have a client on the telephone line while you're recording, or you may be on ISDN doing a live recording session, and right about that time a neighbor starts up a snow blower or a lawn mower. That is the stuff that voice over nightmares are made of.

The goal is to eliminate all outside sound in order to have an empty space to create sound. How you go about finding the best possible space and then making it even better is what we are discussing here.

Since most voice over talent works from home, we all have to find a quiet place at home in order to work. You simply go through your house and you begin to listen like you've never listened before. You've probably never thought about it in that way.

I started searching for my quiet space by going into all my closets. Then I went into every room at different times of day, and I would just listen for the garbage truck to go by, the mail truck, you know, distinctive sounds I recognize. I always have to think about airplanes, too.

Finally, I found the place I thought was the quietest in my house. I'll tell you why it was a good space. It was the closet of the master bedroom, and it was not near an outside wall that is vulnerable to sound. Sounds inside the house and outside the house can interfere with recording.

In your house, see if you can find an interior room or an interior space. Closets are great because there won't be a huge commitment of space, and you really don't need much space anyway. Three feet by five feet is enough, or maybe even less, and you can get set up and start working.

If you can avoid an outside wall it will help the quietness factor. Just realize nobody I know has a 100% sound proof booth or studio. Nobody. You could build it from the ground up, meaning you could start with a special foundation like the big recording studios do. But that is going to be completely cost prohibitive. We all have to start with the best space we have available.

After recording in my bedroom closet for four or five years, I realized it wasn't actually the quietest place in my house. I discovered there was a better space in my basement I could use. So, I stuffed a basement window full of moving blankets to block out some of the exterior sound and that's where I record now, out of my basement.

Currently I use a Whisper Room, which is one of several brands of prefab insulated studios you can set up in your home. Another is called Studio Booth, and there are others. The brand is not so important, but the concept is great.

Consider investing some money in a prefab insulated studio that will help you eliminate even more sound. But you can wait until your voice over business gets rolling to make an investment like this. Just picture me in my bedroom closet for several years if you're feeling anxious now.

My friend, Dave Courvoisier, at Courvo.biz, has some sound blocks that fit together so you can build your own insulated space. They are like Legos made out of soundproofing material. And new products are coming on the market all the time because there's a big demand for sound insulation.

Some people build studios inside their homes by using several layers of drywall. Additional layers of anything will help to block sound. You can reinforce your closet for sound insulation with another layer of drywall, but it won't be 100% soundproof. Nobody can achieve perfection on this issue.

Once you have your quiet space, the next thing is achieving acoustically treated space. It's important to understand the difference. A soundproof space is not a treated space. Soundproof means you're blocking outside noise. Acoustically treated means you're treating the way the sound bounces around inside the room. This is a basic lesson in how sound flows in a space. You really don't need to become an expert on the subject, but you should understand the basic difference.

If you are recording in a room with four steel walls you'll hear a lot of reverb in the recording caused by sound waves bouncing off the hard walls. On the other hand, recording in a room with upholstery and drapery sucks up a lot of the extra sound waves. Depending on the nature of the sound you intend to create you can manipulate your acoustic treatment.

There is a special acoustic foam made specifically for treating walls, but it can be relatively costly. You don't need to spend a lot of money on acoustic wall treatment when you are starting your home studio to do voice over work. I have used such inexpensive methods as foam mattress toppers. Those make great acoustic treatment. Again, they're not soundproofing. They won't keep sound from coming in, but they will control sound created in the room.

Your goal is to create a space where sound waves do not bounce around. You want them to flow gently because that gives you the best recorded voice overs. The insulation we are discussing sucks up extra, bouncy sound waves that detract from your performance. You can even use moving blankets when you start out in a closet or in your basement. The clothes hanging in your closet are actually serving the same purpose for you, too.

You just have to experiment with different methods in the space you have chosen for your studio. Start with your selection of a quiet space, make it as sound proof as possible, and then treat it to control the acoustics, the bouncing sound waves.

There you have a recipe for success in your own home voice over studio. Get this recipe started before you ever think about your recording equipment. First things first – space before equipment.

Now, let's talk about equipment. The single most important piece of equipment you'll purchase is your microphone. The final product, your digital recording will only be as good as your microphone, regardless of everything else. You want to be competitive, but more importantly, you want to get started building your six figure voice over business now. So, I am going to try to balance the importance of buying a good microphone with the reality of grabbing one and getting started right away.

If you really want to produce excellent voice over work you

will need to have a good solid microphone, and by that I mean a large, diaphragm condensing, microphone. I am not endorsing a particular brand and I don't make a kick back of any kind from publishing my suggestions in this book. My comments are not motivated by getting money for myself, but by getting money for you.

There are two basic types of microphones, and you've seen them both in action sometime in your life. You see singers holding dynamic microphones when they are performing on stage. Those microphones are perfect for stage performance because they pick up the full frequency range of the human voice. They are more sensitive and they make the singer sound good.

But for your own purposes, for setting up your home voice over studio and bringing in some real income soon, you need a condenser microphone. Studio mics are more sensitive to surrounding sound, and tend to pick up the nuances of your speaking voice. However, they also pick up more of your neighbor's lawn mower, which is not ideal. Hence, the need for quiet space, first and foremost.

A lot of people ask me about using USB microphones because there are some good ones now. The answer is, I'm sorry to say, USB mics are not a good choice for voice over. Now, USB microphones can be used for auditioning, but I don't use them because I am always thinking about marketing. I am always looking for every possible advantage, for anything I can use to make myself appealing and to make my productions superior. USB mics do not enhance my work in any way.

Sometimes you'll find clients will want to know what microphones you use, and they will not want to work with you if you're using a USB microphone. It is well-known that USB microphones are not as capable of picking up all the nuances and the full dynamic range of your voice. You are marketing all those things, so it's best to use the best dynamic microphone you can afford.

Don't fib, by the way. You will always be discovered. Personally, I might not be able to tell. Even as much as I've done this work, you might be able to fool me, but you will never fool a good studio engineer. Those people know their stuff. To satisfy them with the best possible production work you'll need a good studio microphone. Your condenser microphone will need to be powered, meaning you cannot use a hand held microphone that is operating on a battery.

Powered condenser microphones must be plugged into a mixer with a cord. These studio microphones need to have power fed to them, which is normally accomplished through something called a preamp. A preamp is a dedicated box and the microphone cord plugs into it. A small mixer will have phantom power built in for flexibility.

Since people often ask what brand microphone I use, I'll share that information with you. I use a Neumann, and they are at the very high end of the condenser microphone price range. But even within the Neumann brand there are different price points. Anything that's a Neumann, if it's a large diaphragm condenser, is going to be really good. I use a TLM-103. They just came out with a model called a TLM-102, which is more affordable.

To give you some idea of the current price of Neumann mics, the TLM-103 costs $1,000. I am not suggesting you go out and invest in a microphone that costs $1,000 when you are just starting your voice over business. I am telling you what I use now, after several years of building my reputation.

Another company that I like is Blue Microphones. The best thing about Blue is they offer a broader price range. You might pay $299 for a really good, entry level Blue condenser mic, and you will have a really good microphone. They are completely acceptable.

You will be shopping for a large diaphragm condenser microphone. Within that category you will find a wide price range. If you can afford it, try to start at the $300 level.

Let me tell you a little story about the way I got started, about the microphone I used at first. This may sound like your parents talking, especially when they say, "Let me tell you what I did, but don't you do it." You know, it's the old "do as I say, not as I do" situation we all know well.

Here's what I did. I actually started my voice over career with a microphone that's called a Marshall MXL 2001. Right now you can buy one on eBay for about $60. I recorded for a couple of years with that microphone. A discerning studio engineer might have been able to pick up on the fact I was using a cheap mic, but you need to know I recorded national television ads you've probably seen using that Marshall microphone.

I managed to get by on the cheap, so, I'm not saying it isn't possible to get started with an inexpensive microphone. I did it myself. But I'm suggesting you buy the best microphone you can possibly afford when you start your voice over business because it will give you an advantage now. Check out MusiciansFriend.com and BHPhoto.com for good microphone selections online.

Once again, I will tell you what I did, which doesn't necessarily match up with what I'm telling you to do. I bought all my equipment on eBay. I bought my Neumann microphone slightly used, in excellent condition, for $800 instead of $1,000. And I bought my Aphex 230 preamp there, too. People seem to be interested in what I use every day, which is why I share this information with you. I am not saying these brands are the best or the only ones to buy.

I just know what will work for me and what I need. You will go through a process of discovering those things for yourself over time. There is no reason you have to purchase new equipment, so keep that in mind when you set about to shop for yours. A good condenser microphone and a preamp are the first two items you need in the sound chain, meaning the equipment required to produce voice over recordings. But they are not the only ones.

There are a couple more items you'll need, and the next one is called an audio interface. That's what converts the analog signal, which means the signal that's coming into the microphone, to a digital signal that your computer can recognize and record. An audio interface should not be expensive. I've got one that I've used quite often and I only paid $60 for it. A couple brands you could consider are M-Audio and Lexicon.

An audio interface is also called a sound card; they are basically the same thing. Although computers usually have sound cards built in, they may not be good enough for voice over, which is why you will need to buy an external, USB audio interface to plug into your computer. It will provide a higher quality interface between your microphone and your recording software.

So the next step, and the final piece of equipment you need in your voice over studio, is your computer. I guess that's pretty obvious, but I mention it because some people might be thinking about photos of recording studios in the old days, and the monstrous equipment they've seen in those old photos. It's true, before computers came along this list would have been much longer. But computers have literally replaced a room full of other equipment.

I guess it would be more accurate to say that the final items needed in the sound chain are the recording software and the editing programs in your computer. But, you can see I am trying to keep this list short and simple. The programs you need are not expensive, although you can certainly spend more money along the way. I prefer to stick to a computer and to software that can handle the job with the least expense.

With regard to computers, I use a Mac in my office, but I

record on a PC. And there's a reason for that, which I'll touch on later. I use a Dell Latitude for my voice over recording. I think it's about five years old now. It runs Windows XP, which I have found to be a little more stable than the newer Microsoft operating systems. It works really well with my equipment, and so it doesn't give me any problems. Now you can understand what I mean when I say you can produce high quality voice over work without having the newest or the most expensive equipment.

So, that's the sound chain. Your microphone, your preamp, with or without a mixer in there for headphones, your audio interface or sound card, and your computer with your software. That's your sound chain, in a nutshell. Now we can focus on your recording and editing software, where the final production action takes place.

There seems to be a common misunderstanding among newcomers to voice over that different audio programs produce different sound quality. Truthfully, it doesn't matter at all. No matter what audio program you use, you'll get the same basic quality sound. It's just a matter of how many features are available, what fancy bells and whistles you want on your program.

For Mac users, Garage Band, the recording and editing software included in your Macintosh computer, will work fine for you. Since I'm recording and editing on a PC, I use Adobe Audition. A lot of radio stations use that program, so I'm familiar with it because I come from a radio background. I already knew the program and I'm comfortable using it.

There's a free program available online called Audacity. And another is called Midi Voice Controller for iPads. These free (or nearly free) programs work perfectly for voice over production.

No matter what recording and editing software you select, the program will be working with the sound captured by your microphone. That is why your microphone is all-important. Selection of a microphone is more important than selection of recording and editing software.

You'll find that a preference for any software is primarily a matter of learning and becoming familiar with it, which means you are comfortable using it. I knew how to use Adobe Audition, so that's what I continue to use. Find a program that works for you and stick with it for speed and ease of audio production.

I'd like to briefly explain the basic reason I use a PC in my studio, and that is because I run a little piece of software called Audio TX Communicator. I don't want to confuse the issue at all, but I'll try to explain this simply so it's easy to understand.

I'm not suggesting you do this yet, but I use a technology called ISDN. If you're a beginning voice talent, I highly recommend you do not get it because it's very costly, and unless you absolutely need it, it's a waste of money. I have a very specific reason for using it.

ISDN is a technology that gained popularity back in the 1980s. That decade was its hay day. To make it very simple, it's a way to run high speed data through telephone lines. Stores would use it at the end of the day to send cash register data back to the home office, for example, but it was also great for recording studios. Studios discovered they could do real time recording sessions remotely with other studios having ISDN. It was like a hotline between studios, and it still serves that function today.

I do ISDN sessions with studios in Nashville, New York, Los Angeles and other locations, and it doesn't matter that I'm not there in person because it sounds like I'm there. In other words, I am not recording it myself. I am talking into my home studio microphone and they are recording it on the other end. They have their own directors, producers, and agency people for their various clients. They have more control working with me through ISDN and sometimes that is important.

I can hear them in my headphones, that is how they give me directions. I can't see them, but it is as if I'm sitting right there in the studio with them. Now you know the reasons for use of ISDN, but you also need to know you don't need it to compete when you are starting out. Investing thousands of dollars in an ISDN box, which is actually hardware, is not cost effective until you build up your voice over reputation.

I pay about $45 a month for my ISDN service, and some people pay twice that amount or even more. It costs hundreds of dollars just to set it up initially. If it sounds like I am trying to discourage you about ISDN, it's true. ISDN is a dying technology. Recording studios are still using this technology, but it's getting harder and harder to get the service at all, and the monthly fees are getting higher and higher.

Once you have a great demo, which we will talk about, and you've got your home studio set up for producing excellent quality work, then you simply have to accumulate voice over experience. As you do so, you can compete for better jobs, and then it's more likely you can market yourself to studios using ISDN. If it makes sense for you to get set up to use ISDN in your home studio as I do, more talent agents and websites will represent you because you have the capability to record into markets via ISDN.

My PC runs a program called Audio TX. It is available from a company in England, and it's a software program that helps you avoid spending $3,000 to buy the ISDN box, the piece of hardware I mentioned. Instead, you pay about $800, and you get a dongle, which is a type of USB Key, and a software program to interface with ISDN.

So, that is why I use a PC. To recap, I use a PC because I choose to use special software for ISDN capability. That is my primary reason.

One way your clients can listen in and give you directions on the phone while you are recording is called a phone patch. This is a cheap and easy method for clients to give input that's much cheaper than ISDN, and anyone can do it. Although it can cost several hundred dollars for dedicated hardware programs you can wire into your sound mixer that allow you to plug in your telephone to create a phone patch, it is still less expensive than ISDN.

I'll tell you how I do it, then you can make your own decision about whether you want to invest in phone patch equipment or not. The Audio TX software I mentioned earlier that facilitates ISDN also functions as a phone patch. So, I actually have both options with the same equipment. As you can see, a phone patch may or may not be necessary or practical for you right now.

I probably should leave this next subject out of the book entirely, but here goes - there are times when I don't use phone patch equipment at all. I just use my cell phone. Of course I would never tell my client I'm on a cell phone, and would never do it without two things that you absolutely must have in place before you risk using your cell phone. But the fact is, sometimes I do it.

You need to test to make sure your cell phone does not generate interference in your recording. That is crucial, because any interference in the sound would be the death of your voice over reputation. And the other thing is to make sure you have a good strong signal that won't drop out. You need full bars on your phone. I have both those things so I can use a cell phone if necessary.

Sometimes I just need to be fast, so I give a client my cell phone number. I put one of the ear buds in one of my ears. It has a little speaker in the headphone. Then I put my other headphones on, too. That way, I can talk to the client, and the client can hear me read and give me direction. It's risky, as I said, but it works for me if I absolutely have to do it.

Chapter 12

Workflow In Your Six Figure Voice Over Studio

Let's talk about work flow, about not having extra stuff around. I'm not talking about your personal stuff, only extra stuff in terms of your voice over business.

Over the years, I've developed a system that works well for me. It's very simple. How I store my audio files is foundational, and since they are all stored on the cloud now there is no need for piles of plastic boxes and bins to store CDs or jump drives. That's a big deal.

Cloud storage allows me to work in an uncluttered space and focus entirely on my voice over recordings. That is a luxury that would have been impossible a few years ago. Cloud storage is relatively new, and it's a game-changer for sure.

So, my system for organizing recordings for cloud storage is simple and basic, just like the rest of my studio. I simply create folders on an external hard drive. I use an external hard drive so my recordings are easily accessible, even if my computer crashes, and I label my projects by the year they were recorded.

Right now I'm working out of the 2012 folder. If you were to open up that 2012 folder, next you would see a folder for every current client. Each 2012 client has a separate folder, too.

You would also see 2012 broken down month by month so I can easily find projects. Some people might say that's over the top, a little too organized, but it works for me. That's how I can find what I need quickly.

When you are talking about work flow you really have to start with processing the audio recording, which is called editing. Editing is what happens with your recording, and the final edit is stored in the folders I mentioned.

Before I tell you what I used to do, as regards audio editing when I started building my six figure voice over business, I'm going to tell you what I do now. That is only fair. I make my money when I am talking and recording, so I've hired an assistant to do the audio editing for me.

It will be a good day when you find yourself considering hiring an assistant, too. Although the idea may not appeal to you right now, if you ever start to develop carpal tunnel syndrome while doing all your own editing you might change your mind about getting an editing assistant. That is exactly what happened to me.

Processing audio recordings is critical in delivering a professional product to your client. It is not possible to work as a voice over talent without processing the recordings made in your home studio. This is important to understand.

As we have already discussed, the equipment and software you need are not expensive, and there is plenty of work available. But getting yourself in a position to produce voice over means you are going to be editing your work, too. It is an intrinsic part of the job.

So, in the beginning and until recently, I recorded the audio, I edited the audio and I emailed it to the client. I did it all myself. Keep in mind that a lot of my work is long-form narration; meaning, I may record one, two or three hours of raw audio. Then I have to go back and edit it all. That's many hours of recording and editing combined. And all those hours of editing are hours I am not behind a microphone, which is my primary income producing activity.

Let me mention a really good tip for work flow right now. It's a little trick for ease of audio editing, and making things easier is always welcome, whether you are editing your own work or hiring somebody else to do it.

The bottom line is that we all make mistakes, no matter how much experience we have. Mistakes happen. So, dealing with mistakes is primarily an editing issue. Knowing where to locate the mistakes and edit them out of the final audio is, basically, what editing is all about.

Some people like a feature called a "punch edit", which is included in some recording programs. It allows you to listen to yourself up to the point of a mistake, and then literally punch a button to begin recording over the top of it.

Personally, I think that takes up too much of my time. I've developed my work flow so when I make a mistake I follow up with a clicking sound. That sound creates a spike in the audio that I can see on the screen, and I can see all the mistakes immediately when I review the recording. The spike in the audio signals me to fix a mistake right there.

Some people snap their fingers; some people clap their hands. Just choose a percussion sound of some kind that will create a spike and you'll be able to see where you made mistakes in that recording so you can go back and edit them quickly.

I've come to the place where I can make more money by hiring somebody to edit for me, as I said. So, I hired my daughter as my full-time assistant. She started working for me about four years ago and with her help I can accomplish a lot more work and make a lot more money.

She does all of my editing from the files I record and place in Dropbox. I upload the file to Dropbox and she downloads it onto her computer, edits it and emails it to the client. We work through a lot of email every day. Clients send me emails all day long and we send emails back to them. I need to be able to quickly identify the emails that pertain to the projects I'm working on at the moment.

So, we've created a dedicated email account for my studio, and when a project comes in, it doesn't matter who opens it first. We forward it to the dedicated email account. When I go to my studio and open up my email, all I see are jobs for that day, because everything else has been re-routed elsewhere. This saves a lot of time. This is another way I've been able to eliminate confusion and work in a streamlined manner at the studio.

Chapter 13

Know Your Editing Program
For Top Quality Production

Now we'll go deeper into the subject of editing your audios. As I indicated in the previous chapter, you are going to spend a lot of time editing your recordings. So, the first thing after selecting an editing program, is to invest all the time you need to master it. This investment will repay you over and over because editing is a big part of what you will be doing every day.

As with most businesses, in voice over you'll find that time is money. So you want to become very good, very proficient, and very fast at audio editing. That's why it is so important you dedicate yourself to mastering a program -- whatever it is, it doesn't really matter, just know you need to become good at it. I personally like to stay away from programs that have too many features.

Let me give you an example: Garage Band. For me, Garage Band is not an easy edit, although I'm sure there are some people who have mastered it and find it easy to use. Another example of a program I avoid is Pro Tools. I stay away from it because it's too complex. It's a very good program for audio geek engineers, and for recording, editing and mastering music albums. But that is not what I do.

You just need to find one program you can operate quickly and easily. Pick one and use it. Choose your weapon before entering the fight. We've already discussed the fact that the recording and editing program does not control the final outcome of your voice over work. One program is not going to make you sound better than another program. Your speaking skills and your editing skills are your real money making tools.

At the beginning of every job you will want to find out how your client wants the audio recorded. Be sure to ask about their needs before you get to the editing stage. Generally, your clients will request either a .WAV file if they are working on a PC, or an .AIF file if they are working on a Mac. You'll find very few exceptions to these options for clients desiring uncompressed file formats. In these formats they will not lose any quality, which is important.

Most of my clients actually want them in .MP3, a compressed format. For an MP3 file you'll need to pick the number of megabits per second (mbps) and 192 is high for MP3s, but it is pretty solid. 320 would be comparable to a .WAV or an .AIF, but 192 works and I can't really tell the difference. Just make sure you ask the client for instructions prior to recording so you'll have exactly what is required when the time comes to edit.

I can tell you that 99% of my work is recorded at a 44.1 kHz sample rate, 16 bit depth. I'm not an audio engineer, and the truth is I don't even understand exactly what all that means, except to say the higher the number the better the quality of your audio. Your clients will tell you what they want, and if they don't specify, they will usually tell you to do it as you normally do it. These are good, basic specs to follow.

Once you have your recording, it's a matter of editing out the mistakes. Everyone who does voice overs makes mistakes, and you will make mistakes, too. We all make lots of mistakes. I'm not just referring to stumbling and stammering on occasion, I mean voice work that doesn't hit the mark. When you're recording a commercial you may redo a line 5, 6, 7, 10, 15, or even 20 times. That is not unusual for a voice professional with a focus on excellence.

Once you've completed your recording, you'll look at the screen and what you'll see is a big, long wave form, and you will know there are mistakes you want to fix, so you will want to locate them on the wave as quickly as possible. If you have to go back and listen to the entire recording, it will be a very time-consuming process. This is a good time to remember time is money, and you are only one person with so many hours in the day.

You need to create a visual on that wave so it appears on your screen and you can find it quickly. You want to locate your mistakes quickly and easily in order to fix them. We discussed this trick earlier, but now it will make more sense to you – you want to make a spike on the wave that is easy to see. I make a distinctive clicking sound. That's my sound. Some people snap their fingers or clap their hands to make a spike in the wave. You can do anything that works for you so you can fly through your edits.

At this point, I can take 20 minutes of raw audio and edit out 10, 15 or 20 mistakes in a few minutes. Those spikes in the wave do the trick for me, and you need to find a sound that works for you to locate mistakes and save time editing. You just have to make a sound you use consistently, you can see and quickly identify on your screen. It's as simple as that. Experiment until you find a sound that works for you.

Chapter 14

Your Killer Demo
Is The Key To Getting Jobs

I love talking about the demo because now we're really transitioning into the marketing end of things. And the truth is, before the money comes the marketing. Commit that sentence to memory because you will need to remember it well. Your demo is your number one marketing tool. More than anything else, your demo will decide whether somebody wants to hire you or move on to other voice talent.

Your demo is absolutely the most important element in marketing your voice over business. The demo comes first, and it needs to represent you very, very well. So what is a demo? I'm going to use HGTV as an example because I like it, and because it's all about showcasing. A demo is a way to showcase yourself. When you make a demo you are staging yourself, showing off the best of the best of your voice overs.

In case you're not familiar with HGTV, there are some shows featuring homeowners who are desperate to sell their houses. Some have had houses on the market for a year or two, and they can't sell them and they don't know why. So, the home staging experts walk in the house and they can immediately see the problem. They know how to showcase a home to its best advantage in order to sell it.

That's how it works with your demo. It will be used to stage you in the best possible light to a prospective client. It is designed to show the best work you're capable of performing in a very short time frame.

Most demos today are in the 60- to 90-second range, but demos are getting shorter and shorter all the time, short and fast-moving. Attention spans are growing shorter and there are a lot of young people working at advertising agencies, so your demo only has a few seconds to capture their attention.

To create your demo, you'll want to use short cuts from six to eight different commercials, tightly spliced together in one action-packed bundle, one after another. I'm talking now about a commercial demo because that's the most important one you make.

Although you may have narration demos and audio book demos as well, start with your commercial demo because it will showcase more of who you are and what you're capable of doing. That's where you need to start, and if you don't have actual client work available, you need to improvise.

Record some commercials and find the Money Voice I described in an earlier chapter. Practice and listen to yourself until you can hear it. Then, record and edit snippets together to make a demo. You can build an entire career on a commercial demo without doing anything else. Those six to eight different selections can attract all the work you need.

This is a good time to mention you may want to find a demo coach or a voice coach to work with you and help you identify your Money Voice. Your demo will showcase your talent, and include variations on your Money Voice. It highlights the moments when you sound your best and reveals nuances of your personality and your signature style. It identifies and promotes your skill in delivering a Money Line, which is what commercials are all about.

If this discussion on demos is unfamiliar to you, get online and listen to some commercial demos so you can hear what I'm talking about for yourself. You'll be amazed at how quickly you can size up voice talent in just a few seconds. That's what the client is doing to hire talent, and that's what you must provide to get hired. Go to Voicebank.net and spend some time listening to demos to hear what's out there, and to know what you need to put together so you can compete.

To refresh this subject of your Money Voice, remember I said earlier you'll also begin to explore the areas immediately surrounding it, once you find it. All these areas are the ones you will use on your demo to represent the best of the best of your voice talent. Don't bother to include cuts of other work that simply does not capture your Money Voice.

Your goal is to jump into the demo sounding like a Money Voice immediately, even if your listener doesn't know what a Money Voice is. What matters is that you know, and that you provide your best Money Voice sound immediately. That is where the rubber meets the road. That is what gets your voice over career started and keeps moving.

Personally, I have had five or six different demos over the seven years I've been building my six figure voice over business. I guess that means I produce a new one nearly every year. I continue to grow in my capabilities, and of course I have new work to showcase, so it's worth the investment for me to get new demos made.

I always use a professional demo producer whenever it is time to make a new demo. The first time I recorded a demo I went to Los Angeles. I tried to find the best demo producer I could find. My philosophy is that I will spare no expense on a demo when my career depends on it.

Think of it like a microphone. You know you need to have a good microphone. You need to have a good demo, too, and that means you will need to pay for it. You should consider paying a professional to help you cut your first demo, and every future demo as well.

I remember the producer in Los Angeles stretched me in many different directions as regards my voice over talent. That was part of his job because at the time I didn't have a clue. Since I had worked in radio for a big part of my life, I was a one trick pony for the most part. I had one sound and I stuck to it, because that's the way it works in radio. I mean, we do one thing and that's basically all we do.

But the producer had me doing hyped up voices and he had me doing a low growl. He coached me to explore my talent in much more depth than I had ever explored in the past, and I have to tell you I was surprised to hear what I could do.

A producer will help bring out talent in you; a good coach will bring things out you didn't even know you could do. However, don't put anything on your demo that isn't the very best of your ability. It's not about great versatility, it's about excellence.

Naturally, a question comes up about producing your own demo to save money, especially when you have just invested your money in a good microphone, and your time in learning your recording and editing program, it seems perfectly logical to produce your own demo. But this will be the time to bite the bullet and make another investment.

I always recommend you work with somebody else because it's almost like trying to be your own psychologist. It's just nearly impossible. The fact is you cannot hear yourself the way a professional producer will hear you; nobody can hear the things a good producer can hear.

Regardless of how good you are, you don't hear yourself the way others hear you. That being said, there are elements of my demo I have self-produced over the years to update it. Having become more skilled at what I do as time goes by, instead of flying out to the West Coast or to New York to get 10 seconds of a new demo cut, I've done it myself on occasion. There is a time and a place for everything.

After recording and editing thousands of commercials I've been able to get by with editing my own demo and using it to get agency representation and jobs. But generally speaking, most people can't do that kind of thing. You really need to budget for a professional producer to get your first few demos. The cost will be a small investment in the big picture of your six figure voice over career.

If you're wondering how much you will need to invest in a demo, it will probably run at least $1,000 on the lower end, up to $3,000 or $4,000 at the top. I always tell people to budget about $1,500. You can get a very good demo for $1,500 right now, a world-class demo, so there is really no reason to spend more if you have the right producer.

To find a producer, the best thing to do is to listen to their work and determine which voice over talent has used that person in the past. Have those people been able to gain agency representation? That's the litmus test. If good agents pick you up for their book of voice talent based on your demo, that means you and your demo are both good.

One thing you need to keep in mind is that your demo should represent where you are at this point in your voice over career. I've had people come to me and say they were working with a coach who told them they needed to wait another couple of years before making a demo.

I do not agree. You will be a lot better at voice over in a couple years, but if you have any amount of talent whatsoever I suggest you work with a coach who will record a demo to showcase your capabilities right now. You need to be marketable in order to start your career. And you need a demo to be marketable.

Anyone who has any amount of talent whatsoever can get some coaching and record a competitive demo. It may take some time, and it may take some people a longer time period than others, but it is possible. What you need to understand is that where you are today is not where you will be a year from now, and that's why you will very likely need another new demo to showcase your talent as it grows.

Every year or so, or perhaps even more frequently if you grow fast and revolutionize your entire delivery, you need to be able to show what you've got in order to get the jobs you deserve.

You will undoubtedly discover things about yourself you had no idea you could do. So, as you grow and expand your career your demo should grow and evolve with your capabilities.

Another thing some people tell me is that they don't have any commercial work yet to put in a demo. It doesn't matter now because the way demos work in this fast-paced marketplace, you just have to provide the sound on the demo. It can come from an existing commercial, or it can be staged. That's the whole idea, after all, to stage your talent to get jobs.

For example, I did a national Ford commercial for my demo. Producers and clients are looking for your capabilities because they are shopping for talent with a Money Voice to fill their needs. If you did it in your demo, you can do it for them, too.

Remember to visit Voicebank.net to hear what's out there and to know what will be expected of you as well. Anyone can listen to demos on Voicebank, but the only way to post your own demo is through an agent. You must have agency representation to post on that website.

I encourage you to go there and type in my name, Bill De-Wees, and you will hear my current demo. Listen to other demos, too. Spend some time experiencing what producers and directors and all your prospective clients experience when they are shopping for voice talent.

That is how you will get a handle on the state of the industry in terms of what other voice over talent are doing. And that is what you need to know in order to be competitive.

Chapter 15

Your Hard-Working Website

After your killer demo, your second most important marketing tool is your website. The whole reason for it, the one-and-only purpose of your voice over website, is to get people to listen to your demo. Your website is where your demo lives online. It is how you provide an address for people to find your demo on the web when they want to hear it.

Your website is where you will send people to listen to your demo. Build your website with this primary objective in mind, and don't get distracted by what lots of people will tell you about making money with websites. Stick to your primary business and your primary goal with this website for your business – getting people to hire you when they hear your demo. That's it.

That is your primary objective because that's what will seal the deal. When people listen to your demo, they will either hire you or give you a chance to audition, or not, based on the strength of your demo. Your website is the place you showcase the demo that stages your talents. Don't try to complicate it or make it do more than one thing. Just make sure your website does one thing well.

The next point I want to make is that you need to have a dedicated domain, your own domain name. One of the biggest mistakes I see in voice over websites I visit before a consultation is the lack of a dedicated domain address. Your demo on Voice123.com or Voices.com is not your own website. Without your own website, your own address where your demo lives on the web, you're just not a serious player.

Think about it this way, why would you send somebody to a website that has 20,000 other voices to choose from? Essentially, by sending a potential client to those two sites or other sites like them you are sending them straight to your competition. That is not a good thing at all. You want to capture their attention. Sending them to your competition can be distracting and disastrous to your purpose.

Right now you may be wondering: How do I get a domain name? How do I set up a website? Is it easy? What should I do? When I had all these questions at first, I was pretty intimidated. I had never set up a domain before. It's actually very easy. You can go to smartdomaintool.com and find everything you need to get started without a lot of expense. It's a cheap way to get your own domain name and a host for your website. It's kind of a one-stop shop.

You'll find all the tools you need to build your own website right there, as well as your own domain name, your address on the web. I always recommend using your own name; I use BillDewees.com because I want people to remember my name. I want everything to direct attention to me, to my name.

When you create your website, simple is better. I have a couple of mantras that won't surprise you at this point - less is more and simple is better. Squeezing more copy into a commercial does not make it more effective, and the same is true of websites, too. Squeezing more on the page, especially the first page, the home page of your website, does not make it more effective.

Always stop and think about what you are really trying to accomplish. You want the person, any person on your website to listen to your demo. That's it. You don't want them to do anything else. Don't give them any distractions and you will accomplish this purpose. That is all they can do, so it is what they will do.

Ultimately, you want them to contact you and hire you, so you have to provide a way for them to do that. They have to be able to contact you to hire you and to pay you. Getting paid is the end goal, but that won't happen until you get hired. So, getting hired is the first and most important goal of your demo on your website.

You want to make sure your name is highly visible and looks professional It should look clean and uncluttered. It should be easy to read. I want people to see my name so I put it up at the top of my website. And I want them to see my demos on the home page. They should be able to play the demos right on the home page. Trust me, if they have to look around for your demos, if they have to click to one more page, you're defeated before you even begin.

If visitors to your website have to start clicking around to find your demos, forget it. The reality is that they have literally hundreds of other people they can hire for this job. They don't need to waste their time trying to locate your demos.

I recommend using a professional to design your website for you. Yet again, professionalism pays off. If you choose to build your website yourself, use some really clean graphics that look fresh and up-to-date. You don't have to make it elaborate or flashy, but it needs to be very clean. Remember my mantras – less is more and simple is better. Use these concepts to make money with your voice over website.

When you visit my website at BillDeWees.com you will note I also feature a list of clients and client logos. I can do this now, but that was not always the case. And the only reason I take up space with that information is to get people to listen to my demos. Everything is designed to lead to that. If you are just starting out you won't have a client list and a collection of client logos anyway, so don't worry about them.

I started with everything except a client list on my website. If you can get some testimonials from clients now, that's the next best thing. I waited until I had what is called "credits". The names and logos of well-known clients definitely attracts more clients, but people will listen to your demos without credits on your website. It's just a way to add credibility to what you have already showcased – your killer demo.

Sooner or later you will be hired to do voice over work for a company people will recognize by name. But until then, don't use unrecognizable names or logos. Don't use Bob's Used Cars. Make sure you only use name brands on your website.

And by the way, just because I have Sears on my website doesn't mean I recorded a national television commercial for Sears. I recorded an in-store commercial they used in their home and garden section. But it's still Sears so I list them and include their logo.

I did not record a Microsoft national television commercial, but I did produce training materials for Office 10. Those are credits. They count. It doesn't matter if you're the voice over on a corporate telephone system or if you're on a national television commercial. Those are all credits and you can use them to your advantage on your own website.

Providing a client list and client logos is proof those companies believed in you and hired you. Most clients want to be reassured as they make their decisions. Most people don't make decisions because they think it is going to be great and awesome to hire Bill DeWees. They want to use Bill DeWees because they know they will not be making a stupid mistake that will embarrass them. When they see the companies listed on my website and know those companies trusted my work, they are reassured about trusting my work, too.

Clients are thinking they can trust me if Travelers Insurance, Microsoft, Dell, HP and Cisco have trusted me. Those companies hired Bill DeWees and he didn't screw up, so he probably won't screw up too badly or embarrass them now. You have to understand that's what most people are trying to avoid. They're trying to avoid the pain of embarrassment when they're picking voice talent. They want you to sound good so they will look good.

Your website must be designed to create credibility, and it must be easy to find and to use. Your domain name should make it easy to find you, and your home page should make it easy to hear your demos immediately. All that should encourage people trust you, contact you and hire you. It's that simple.

Chapter 16

My Proven Marketing Philosophy Can Be Yours Now

I have a marketing philosophy, and it is unique to me, but I am offering to give it to you now. I suggest you accept it and use it, because it can literally save your life as voice over talent.

What I've found through coaching voice over and working with other talent is that most people are busy thinking about their performance. They are consumed with perfecting their performance. Rarely are they thinking in terms of building a business.

So the first thing, if you want to make good money as voice talent, is to start thinking like a business person as well as a performer. You absolutely must be able to do both in the current marketplace. Most people don't fail because they lack talent, they fail because they don't have a clue how to market themselves and to make money. Talent alone will not create success.

I have observed that other voice over coaches seem to focus on the performance side of this business, and not on the marketing side of it. You can find lots of material on the subject of voice over performance, but very little on marketing yourself as voice over talent. Oh, maybe you'll find a suggestion to send out some postcards or some emails. And maybe you will be encouraged to make a few phone calls. But that is not enough these days.

Truthfully, I don't care how good you are if you can't make money. What's the point? Who cares? I really do love what I do. I love getting behind the microphone and recording, but I will only do it if I can make money doing it. And I aim to make good money doing it or I'll pass.

If I cannot make good money consistently, day in and day out, I'd better find something else to do in order to support myself and my family. The voice over business provides very well for me and my family, but that is primarily because I obsess on constantly marketing myself. I never slack off.

It seems to me most people approach a voice over business like winning the lottery, as if they think maybe voice over will provide a good retirement plan. This is just like people who think the lottery is a good retirement plan. They go out and buy a couple of lottery tickets every week, hoping they will hit the jackpot.

Most voice over talent approaches marketing as if they're playing the lottery. They get an agent, or more than one agent. They fill a few auditions and keep relying on their agents, hoping that something will eventually hit big. They hit for home runs only, and they wait around a lot.

But I'm playing small ball, although occasionally I hit a big one. I'll be honest with you, it's not the sexiest or the most glamorous way to approach the voice over business at all. But I am not in this business to be glamorous. I am in it to make money, all day, every day.

There isn't much voice over talent that actually lead a glamorous life. I mean, it is work. It is constant, consistent work. And if it is not a constant stream of work, there is no constant stream of income.

Back to baseball for a moment - hitting singles can win the game. It is basic, and it is within your grasp today. You know you can do it now; you can make money doing it now and it all begins with a high volume approach. I market constantly and I have done so since I started.

When I first started I marketed like a maniac and I tried everything. I discovered there are several ways to market myself effectively, as long as I am willing to hit singles and keep making progress. I take the high volume approach to build my portfolio and my six figure business.

Now, I realize if you look at my current book of business you're going to see jobs in there that are pretty sizable. You would see some big clients and big jobs every month on my calendar. But they are in the minority.

You will discover that a majority of my clients are not big. Not every job I get pays me thousands of dollars. As a matter of fact, most of the jobs I get do not pay me thousands of dollars. Most of my jobs are in the hundreds of dollars each. This may be a sobering reality, but it also puts my advice in sharp perspective. I practice what I preach, and I do it every day.

You may be shocked to hear that craigslist.org is my biggest source of leads. That is a surprising statistic, I'll admit. In fact, that may go completely against the things you have heard from other people in the area of voice over marketing. Many people would say that craigslist ads are not worth contacting, that it's beneath them to bother with it. That's fine with me because it leaves more low-hanging fruit for me to pick.

I hear people say, "I won't turn on my microphone for less than $150." And I say, "Great. That leaves more work for me!" Are you getting the picture, folks? I will stoop down to pick up a dollar off the sidewalk when others refuse to do so. They are looking for hundred dollar bills, and they are too busy looking for those hundreds to make any money.

I will gladly pick up dollar bills all day long. When I first started my goal was to make $200 a day, and I quickly achieved that goal. Now my goal is $1,000 a day. And if that means I need to complete ten jobs to accomplish that goal, I'll do it. If I need to record one job to do it, so be it. I don't really care. I want to make money; I am not in this business to boost my pride.

More than half of my clients are repeat customers, I would say closer to 75% now. You always want to attract new customers, so you always have to be marketing yourself to some extent, but I am to the point that most of my time is spent recording instead of marketing.

Maybe a better way to say it would be that my marketing has

changed. An evolution takes place as you build a voice over business. When you first start out it's all about getting new clients because you don't have a choice.

But, as you build your client list you begin to market to those same people. You keep in touch and make sure they don't forget about your excellent work in the past. Your marketing is more about keeping in touch, and reminding them that you are ready to provide excellent results whenever they need some. You want to be the first person they call.

I primarily market to my clients now, and I try to make sure they hear from me at least once a month. I might call or send an email to say, "Thanks for your business. I really appreciate the fact that you hire me, and whenever there is anything I can do for you please let me know." I've been known to send video emails. The particular method you use isn't as important as the fact you are reaching out to make sure you stay top-of-mind in their busy lives.

When I first started I used craigslist a lot. And I did a lot of auditioning on Voices.com and Voice123.com, the big pay-to-play websites. I also called and emailed studios that specialize in high-volume, low-cost commercials for radio and television stations. I marketed myself to a lot of video production houses, and I still do that. But now I spend now more of my time marketing to my own clients.

Whenever I decide to send a video email I use SmartVideo-MailTool.com and it is really a great way to send a personal message to people you already know. I'm always looking for ways to get attention. Everybody is bombarded by information all day long, online and offline, too. So you have to find a way to cut through the clutter.

I'll do anything reasonable to get attention because I know if I get a client or a prospective client to think about me, I can rise to the top. The goal of marketing is getting people to act once you get their attention, because the old saying has never been more true, "Out of sight, out of mind." You have to get their attention to get them to hire you. Getting attention gets jobs.

Make sure you pay attention to the fact that people simply won't remember you without helping them remember you. And it's not because you're a bad person or you're boring or you're not memorable, it's just that they are busy and distracted thousands of times per day. You are not on their radar screens without putting effort into being there.

So, how can you get on their radar consistently? If you want to be hired consistently you have to stay on radar screens consistently. Video email has become a favorite of mine because it's still relatively novel in most people's inboxes, and it causes them to see my smiling face saying, "Hey, I just wanted to say thank you. I'm checking in to see if you need some more voice over work now." Again, the method is not as important as the fact that you do something, anything, to stay in front of your clients.

Again, if you look at my book of business you're going to see lower paying clients, but not just any lower paying clients. I take clients who do a large volume of work with me. Each individual recording might not bring in a lot of money, but the number of recordings I do for the same client makes up for it. I have clients who pay me several thousand dollars each month on a regular basis, so I am going to give them a much better rate than somebody who hires me once a year.

I'm happy to work for that lower rate because it's guaranteed income for me. It's just smart business, in my mind. And in reality, that's the way I make a pretty good living doing voice overs. You might say I welcome the mid-pay clients in order to solidify my income stream.

I love those bigger jobs that pay me $1,000 or more per project. But earning $1,000 per day, one way or the other, is not bad. I find ways to make $1,000 a day now, and aim to make more per day in the future.

Coaches who teach you to hold out for the big gig are not

keeping up with the new model and the reality of the times. There are only so many big jobs out there, but there are a ton of jobs that are slightly smaller, meaning they pay anywhere from $100 to maybe $500 each. And there are scads of even smaller jobs that pay $50 here or $75 there. If you are willing accept assignments at these rates on a daily or a weekly basis, my advice is simple – take those jobs.

If you have any degree of competence in doing voice overs, you will build an income in your own business by being willing to take the projects that are available. Voice over work is not exactly ditch digging, all things considered. There are many things you could do to earn a living that are much harder than voice over. True? Maybe you are doing those things to earn a living now, in fact.

I'll take consistent money all day long because it's a stable source of income for me. This is what I call the portfolio approach to marketing. I am building my portfolio of clients and marketing to them to build my business. I am willing to do a little bit of everything.

When people ask, "Won't that hurt you? Isn't that unfair?" I say, "Absolutely not." Recording a commercial for a small radio station in Paducah, Kentucky, is not the same as a commercial for a radio station in Los Angeles or New York. The economics of the clients are completely different.

How can I expect a client in a small market to pay me $500 for a spot when that might be all they earn from running the spot? There are basic economics involved, and I choose to pay attention to my bottom line by paying attention to my clients' bottom lines. Unfortunately, most voice over talent is mired in professional pride, holding out for a dollar amount per job or per hour to establish value.

I see it differently. If I am not generating value for my client, I have no value. It's that simple. Basically, you have to swallow your pride because if you think you are above certain jobs, you are going to starve while you wait for great jobs to come along. You will get great jobs by being willing to fulfill clients' needs for lower paying jobs along the way.

This is my philosophy, this is my approach. This is what allows me to make a multiple six figure income. I can say for certain I am in the top 1% of earners in the voice over business. In other words, my philosophy is working for me.

Maybe I should throw in something else right about now, too. Some people say it hurts the voice over industry if I take a lower paying job. They say it lowers the bar for everyone else. This is simply inaccurate. The market will bear only so much expense on voice talent. Ignoring this fact leads to unemployment as a voice over talent, I assure you.

You value is exactly and precisely what a client is willing to pay you right now, bearing in mind that amount can change over time. But right now, that is how much you're worth. And I mean, in terms of the marketplace, it's not a penny more, not a penny less. In a free market system, you can take it or leave it. It is completely up to you. And never forget, if somebody else leaves it, I have an opportunity to take it, to complete a job that may very well lead to a better paying job.

All this might sound like I take anything that comes along, but that's not true. I only take jobs if I can schedule the time and if the particular client is likely to turn into a good, repeat client for me. I only like to work with good clients, which means clients who pay on time and who are easy to work with.

Sooner or later, we all experience our share of clients who are far more trouble than they are worth. I don't take on those clients anymore. Or, if I have clients who are difficult to work with, I fire them.

As regards finding new clients to replace them, I endeavor to overwhelm the market. I look at everything. I'm still looking at craigslist and I'm marketing myself to video production companies. I have outsourced that marketing task, as a matter of fact.

I've hired somebody who markets to production companies for me on a commission basis. This arrangement is cost effective for me because you usually have to contact hundreds of companies to get a response. I make my money producing voice over, so I can hire an assistant to market to video production companies for me, allowing me to spend my time working.

Let me make sure you don't misunderstand anything I'm saying about employees or outsourcing right now; I do not have a lot of employees. I hire my daughter to edit my audio recordings and to communicate with clients.

She and I both wade through emails and voice messages to clean out everything that is not work-related. Nobody else works for me at my studio. And I have a virtual assistant who works online to market me to video production companies. That's it. There's nobody else. I have several talent agents, but they are definitely not employees. My agents pay me, I don't pay them.

I outsourced my marketing to video production companies because it is very easy. I created a template email, and my assistant simply goes to Mandy.com and sends out 20 - 50 emails at a time to companies listed on that site.

Mandy.com is the most comprehensive directory of video production companies in the world. Hundreds of video companies per week are hearing from me, and anytime I get a positive response, the contact name goes into my database and I follow up.

I continue to email those contacts once a month in order to stay on their radar screen. Honestly, I don't get many responses from this process. It's a numbers game. If you've been in sales you know how it works. You don't get many jobs from this system, but in reality, I don't need most of those jobs. All I'm fishing for is a handful of good clients and that keeps me rocking and rolling, every week, every month, every year.

Chapter 17

My Evergreen Marketing Strategy – Take Two

I am going to elaborate on my marketing strategy now, just to emphasize the importance I place on marketing activities in the big picture. It is not a coincidence I am making a good living with my voice over business. It is intentional. I do whatever it takes to stay busy recording client work in order to get paid.

We addressed my philosophy on marketing and the mindset I prefer, and why I prefer it. Now I want to share more about the practical application of my philosophy and my mindset, which you are free to adopt as your own at any point. That is the purpose of this book – to encourage you to develop a successful mindset and get into action.

To market yourself effectively, you have to go where the clients are. In the old model, as we've discussed, that meant showing up in person for auditions. In the new model, things have changed dramatically. Instant communication and information allows anyone to get in touch with potential clients without using an agent.

That being said, it is still wise to have one or more agents, because agents do a couple of things for you. Number one, they lend credibility to you because they vet their talent. In theory, the fact you are represented by a talent agent means you are good. Having an agent works in your favor for that level of credibility. Number two, agents are the gatekeepers for a lot of the really high paying, high profile jobs.

You'll remember it is much easier for big clients to work with a few agents than thousands of aspiring voice over talent. So, there will always be jobs that can only be accessed through an agent. When you work with an agent it's important to know some are exclusive and some are non-exclusive. My suggestion is to try to work with non-exclusive agents so you can have as many as possible. No agent knows about every voice over job on the market.

As I also said earlier, I've got 16 agents right now. That gives me access to a lot of auditions. But if I were to rely solely on my agents for my income I would make less than 2% of what I currently earn. I am my own best agent, as you can quickly see. None of my agents would be pleased to hear I routinely get jobs on craigslist, but that doesn't stop me. I do what I need to do in order to produce work for clients and get paid consistently.

Basically, whatever you do, whatever marketing tools you employ, whatever strategies and tactics you utilize, do them consistently. Don't approach your marketing like you play the lottery, getting discouraged when you don't win right away. You may not hit 99 times out of 100, but that 100th time can make you a winner. If you need five jobs this week, you have to stay in the game. You have to play, and you have to think of it this way to win.

I can go for days, even weeks without finding jobs on craigslist. I've gone for a couple of months without finding a good gig there. But I don't want to miss it on the day a good job finally pops up, because I have been investing my time and because I know that even a small job can lead to bigger jobs in the future.

Once again, don't tell my agents, but I've landed some phenomenal clients and I've made a lot of money through craigslist. I've been signed with some really good agents through craigslist, too. Sometimes agencies will advertise on craigslist when they're looking to expand their talent rosters, and they will want to hear demos at that point.

I've mentioned there are many freelance sites now, and given you some suggestions of sites to use. The number of sites where you can post your demo is huge, and growing. Do a Google search on freelance voice over and you'll see a dozen or more sites pop up.

I don't have to use this method now, but if I were just starting out I certainly would do it. I would do everything, all the time, in order to get work. Besides Voices.com and Voice123.com you might want to check out Bodalgo.com, which is based in Europe.

Generally, you will pay an annual fee to post your demo on these sites, and the more you pay, the more auditions you'll be able to access. You may have to pay $300 per year for some sites, depending on the level of access you desire.

These sites are not agencies. You never pay for an agent; an agent pays you, and keeps a percentage of what you earn as his or her fee. Don't forget that because sometimes I hear about unscrupulous agencies trying to obtain money from aspiring voice over talent just starting out.

Once you choose the sites and post your demo, in theory you can submit hundreds of auditions over the course of a year. When I first started out I did a lot of auditioning through pay-to-play sites. And you'll recall I have a coaching student who did the same thing for a long time before he broke through and finally got good, steady business from repeat clients.

I've mentioned the production companies that specialize in creating low-cost radio and television ads. Each of these companies has its own talent rosters, so you have to get on their rosters to get their work. I found many of the production companies I'm working with right now by entering the words "talent roster" in a Google search.

I submitted my demo to them after finding instructions on their website as to where I could send my demo for consideration. It still works that way now. Of course, they may or may not have a spot for you right when you submit your demo. Think of it this way - an agency or a production company is usually looking for a broad range of voices, but if they have somebody who fits your typical style they may not need you right now.

The general rule is that you can resubmit your materials about once every six months without appearing obnoxious. You just have to realize you may not get jobs immediately. You need to keep submitting your demo about every six months, to get it back in front of possible clients and agencies again and again. Market yourself to video production companies, too, as I explained previously

Besides Mandy.com, which is a great source for contacting video production companies, there are literally thousands of other sites that list companies in the business of producing television commercials and corporate videos. I cannot emphasize enough the goldmine of opportunities for voice over work that is currently available through production companies.

Here's something else to keep in mind, a bit of marketing strategy I use whenever possible. Instead of marketing directly to clients, I market myself to the agencies and production companies already marketing to prospective and current clients. In other words, I go to the production companies and studios that are spending money to attract business, and I make sure they remember me whenever they need voice talent over for their projects.

The companies that create radio commercials, television commercials and corporate videos already have a marketing team working non-stop to get clients. They have sales people and they have leads. Working with production companies gives me more than just one client; it gives me access to 50 or 100 clients or more right off the bat. So, I focus on sending a link to my website to production companies as a primary marketing strategy.

You may be wondering how I feel about social media such as LinkedIn, Facebook, Twitter and other platforms. There is an ongoing discussion within the voice over industry about the value of using social media for marketing, and whether it has been, or will ever be, effective. I hear some people have made contacts and picked up voice over work through social media. But I have not. Not once.

I use social media in a different way. I don't think social media is the most effective or the fastest way to get work because the methods I have been sharing are much more effective for me. On the other hand, I think social media is something to watch, especially LinkedIn. That forum could become valuable.

For my business now, at this stage of my career, LinkedIn is not as valuable as all of the other marketing I do. Right now I use it as a marketing tool, but only to keep my name in front of people using that site.

I link to a client whenever possible, and sometimes I send out information on a project I'm working on, or voice over information I consider interesting. Again, I don't want to drop off the radar screen, I want to pop up on the radar wherever and whenever I can. So I'm not marketing for work, I'm marketing for visibility on social media.

One thing many people have learned the hard way, and I mean to the detriment of their voice over careers, is something you must understand about your social media postings. When I talk about marketing for visibility, be careful to avoid marketing yourself in a way that gives a bad impression. Don't frequent social media sites to share personal information or negative comments that could come back to haunt you.

Even using social media in a positive way can create a condition I call over exposure. Frankly, people can get tired of seeing your name and your constant commentary. They can draw the conclusion you must be bored and desperate for work if you have enough time available to post trivial comments online all the time. I don't want to give that impression, and the truth is I don't have the time.

Here's an example of something I posted that should bring the kind of attention I want from social media. Recently, I produced a trailer for Madagascar III, the movie. I made a brief mention of it on Twitter, Facebook and LinkedIn saying, "Today I'm working on the trailer for Madagascar III." That comment is interesting and it makes me look good. It works to enhance my reputation and my business.

But posting comments like that one too often can sound like bragging. I don't want to sound arrogant, so I keep my postings short and infrequent. My goal is to attract attention in a good way, and to jog the memories of past and potential clients in order to get work. That's it. I'm not on social media sites for any other reason.

Chapter 18

Marketing Execution For
Voice Over Success – Follow Me

To put your marketing activities into clear perspective, you need to understand that in the beginning there will be much more marketing going on than recording and editing. You have to market to get to the work. I call it the 90/10 rule: Expect to do 90 % marketing and 10 % voice over work when you first start your business.

And, 90/10 is what you can expect when things are going well. The percentage of marketing activities may even exceed 90% in many cases, so don't be surprised. But it doesn't really matter. The point is, you need to market yourself in all the ways we've been discussing. You do all the right things, or as many of them as possible. You keep on doing the right things. You keep on keeping on, and sooner or later you begin to pick up clients. You WILL get jobs.

The downside to marketing successfully and getting a lot of work is you may accidentally abandon your marketing efforts when you are busy. Once you complete all the jobs in your queue, suddenly you may find yourself out of work.

Dropping your marketing efforts because you are busy recording and editing is a big mistake we all make until we suffer the consequences. It's a boom or bust cycle, and it is not the way to build consistent business. Because when the boom or bust cycle happens in terms of your work, it also happens in terms of your income.

Once you start making some money, don't spend it all. Budget for the inevitable boom or bust cycles, and for the ups and downs that may occur as you build your business. You have to be working consistently to have consistent income. This is proactive business planning. Make sure you have some money saved in case you need it.

I have managed to build a consistent income over the years. This is not bragging, it's the plain truth - I've never had a bad income month in seven years. Never. Once I got up and rolling, after the first few months I haven't had a bad month.

Now that I think about it, I've never had a bad income week either. I rarely have a bad day. I've never had a day when I didn't earn some income. I've never had a zero day. And the reason for this good luck is not luck at all. It is the result of constant, relentless marketing efforts. I have constant income because I market myself constantly.

To put my income stream into perspective, on my best day ever I earned $2,000. And my best week ever was about $6,500. My best month was about $22,000, best I can recall. I normally calculate my income in terms of days and weeks; keeping a close watch on the numbers keeps me motivated.

I am interested in what will happen, not what could happen, or what might happen. I am not waiting for my 16 agents to call with jobs for me. I am out there hustling jobs, every day. This is the quality that sets me apart from other voice over talent and from other voice over coaches. Most people in the voice over business are not getting consistent income like this, and most coaches are not teaching their students how to get consistent income like this.

My approach to building income is not considered desirable by anybody who is holding out for high paying jobs. Those people are interested in peer recognition and their own opinions. They are the same people who love awards.

All I care about is the return on my investment – ROI. I don't care about winning awards. My bank accounts are my rewards. And I don't care if anyone knows how much money I make. I'm not making my money to impress others.

There's no doubt that my MBA and background working in

various businesses give me an advantage over people who are primarily artists and performers. I am an artist and a performer, but that is not how I identify myself.

I think of myself as a businessman, and I happen to be in the voice over business. I like business. I am successful in my business. I am not in this for people to admire me or my artistic work. I am in my voice over business to make money. I perform to make money, not to satisfy my ego.

I am not fantasizing about being a successful actor. In fact, my approach to voice over is completely the opposite. I am interested in the art of making money, not becoming the next George Clooney or Samuel L. Jackson.

I am not dreaming about being a big star, or getting well-known. I don't care about Academy Awards or any other awards, for that matter. I care about making as much money as possible in my voice over business and I do whatever it takes to make it happen.

You might say that my approach is very blue collar. Git'er done. Not in terms of income, of course. Mine is not a blue collar income, but my work ethic and the way that I approach each job is very blue collar.

I grind out the work, and I never stop marketing because I need to be able to grind it out again tomorrow and the next day, etc. That attitude is what sets me apart from other voice over talent I know.

As I've said, the voice over business is not glamorous or sexy. It is consistent marketing, recording and editing. Rinse and repeat, and don't stop there. Do it all again tomorrow if you want to build a six figure income.

To pinpoint another detail regarding marketing, I am always thinking about who to contact next. Generally speaking, Casting Director is going to be the job title of the person you need to contact. That is the job title at television stations and production companies. Despite the fact that I know this is probably the job title of the person I need to contact, sometimes I play ignorant and it works to my advantage.

Sometimes I'll call and ask, "Can I talk to the person in charge of working with voice talent?" Whoever answers the phone always knows who that person is. Surprisingly, eight times out of 10 it's the same person I'm already talking to, the one who answers the telephone.

So, it's very easy to get to the decision maker in most cases. If you're marketing to radio stations, the Program Director is the more likely job title, but asking for the Casting Director is universal, and it works pretty much everywhere.

With regard to making phone calls or sending emails, I use both. I've done a lot of cold calling, and it has been very effective for me. I like cold calling – well, let me back up. I don't like to do it. Nobody actually likes cold calling, which means you are calling a place where nobody knows you yet.

But I like the results it gets. I know this is hard to believe, but I have never had a negative experience making cold calls to get voice over work. They are always looking for good voice talent, so it's not like I'm trying to sell ice cubes to Eskimos.

Remember, when you are cold calling you should only have one primary goal. And my goal is always get them to listen to my demo. That's it. I'm not calling anybody to chat. It's just the same as my website.

My website has the same goal – promoting my demo. I am cold calling to find the right person to send him to my demo on my website online. I am calling to get the name of that person for my records, yes, but the only reason I want the contact information is to drive him straight to my website demo.

I can never control whether anyone will agree to hire me, but if I can get someone to agree to listen to my demo, I win. Again, I usually play really stupid, as though I don't know what's going on. I'll say, "I'm a full-time voice talent from the Chicago area." Or, sometimes I don't even mention my location because it really doesn't matter where I live. Location is basically irrelevant.

And then I'll say, "Can I speak to the person in charge of working with voice talent?" And more times than not I'll hear this reply, "Yeah, that would be me. Can I help you?" Then I say, "Yeah, are you accepting demos right now from voice talent?"

You might want to write that last sentence on a slip of paper and keep it in your wallet. That's my big question, and it works. Nine times out of 10 I will hear, "Yeah, sure." And then I'll say, "Would you prefer a link to my website, or can I send you an MP3?" I don't like to send attachments to emails because oftentimes they go to junk or are deleted, so don't offer that option.

When I ask for their preference they will normally say, "Yes, send me a link to your website." People don't like to deal with files attached to emails. I get their email address at that point and I send them a link to my website. That's how the magic works, such as it is. You can see there is really no magic at all, just persistent, focused effort. And that's how it works.

It may be hard to believe, but I've never had somebody say, "You know, don't ever call me again. Leave me alone. No, we never use voice talent." That has never happened. I've never had a bad experience making calls like these. Naturally, I allocated more time to cold calling in the beginning of my voice over career. But I still do it because it works.

Once I have an email address, I can use it once a month or so to keep my name on the radar screen. And once I have a client, I'll send them video emails, perhaps thanking them or just saying hi, to keep my face in front of them.

Consistency is the key. Consistency means doing it and continuing to do it. It's the execution. It's always execution. Execution, execution, execution. My marketing model is relentless, no matter how much money I earn. I will never stop marketing, and

I make sure other people know my non-stop marketing efforts are the reason for my success in voice over.

In other words, if I sit down with you – let's say you are set up and working as voice talent - and you say, "Bill, man, I'm struggling." Before we ever get into a discussion I will know your problem is an execution problem. I'll say, "Okay, who are you contacting?"

I will know it's not the words you are saying or not saying. We can fumble around for words because there are no magic words at all. You just find a way to get to the main point, which is, "Hey, are you accepting voice over demos?" It's not rocket science or brain surgery. And it's not waiting for your agent to call with auditions, either.

It's just you on your phone making calls because your life depends on it. The life of your voice over business depends on it, that's for sure. I often hear, "I did that for a few months and it just didn't work out." I hear that about all aspects of marketing, but mostly about cold calling.

If you feel like nothing is working out, you are probably doing it right. That is exactly what happens in the beginning. I received an email a few days ago that makes this point perfectly. This is a true story and it shows you exactly what I am describing about relentless marketing.

I received an email from a guy I worked with who just about gave up on his voice over career. He had submitted 150 auditions, but hadn't landed a job. I worked with him and I knew he was doing the right stuff. And I knew he had a good demo. I knew he was marketable. I knew it was just a matter of time. And so I said, "Joe, don't stop. You're doing the right stuff. Just keep doing it." All of a sudden it all opened up. He got jobs.

I've worked in sales in the past, and by that I mean I've had several sales jobs. I remember sales managers always saying, "The best time to make a call is right after a sale." The reason it is the best time to call is because your attitude is different. You are not expecting somebody to say no and you're more upbeat and you're relatively relaxed. That's the thing. It's not about selling people on me and getting them to hire me immediately. All I'm trying to do is get them to listen to my demo.

Now, in order to get people to listen to my demo consistently, I have a routine. You will have to develop some kind of a routine, too. Your routine is basically your marketing plan. It's part of your business plan. I am not talking about creating an elaborate document, but assessing your strengths and weaknesses.

It is often called a SWOT analysis, which is an acronym for Strengths, Weaknesses, Opportunities and Threats. It is a great way to begin to understand yourself, what you have now, how to leverage what you have now, and how to prepare for the future.

Establishing your routine doesn't require a formal marketing or business plan. It requires having a good website and a killer demo. Establishing your routine helps you set up a pattern of behavior so you can get into action. You can perform when you get jobs, and you can commit to making phone calls, sending emails, and scouring the internet for opportunities relentlessly, every day.

When I first started, I spent about 95% of my time marketing for the first month or two. I was always marketing, and occasionally I was getting a job. The thrill of getting the job was more fun than the job itself. You will get to that point, too. It's a thrill to get a new client. And now, almost seven years later, I spend 95% of my time recording and 5% marketing.

Just for the sake of explanation, I could say the percentages were probably 80/20 the second year, and 60/40 the following year, or something like that. And after about three years it was 50/50. But it never stops.

The 5% of my time I spend marketing myself now is in addition to the virtual assistant who promotes me to production companies, and to the regular client communication that keeps me on my clients' radar screens. My regular communication works just like marketing for me at this point.

If somewhere in the back of your mind you are wondering, while you are reading this book, "Am I good enough?", you are asking the wrong question. It is such a common issue we need to talk about it now. The answer is, "Yes, you are good enough. Or you can be with some training."

While I certainly hope that brings you some relief, you have to understand that getting good and then spending time and money to get better doesn't automatically create work. What creates work is your relentless marketing efforts. It's doing whatever it takes to get people to listen to your demo. That comes before the job offers.

One of the best things I ever experienced that really taught me about sales was a door-to-door sales job I worked when I was in college. I knocked on the doors of complete strangers and asked if they would like to buy a Bible, or a magazine subscription or some other book. We sold a variety of books. I was very shy, and for some reason I signed up for this sales opportunity, although I'd never done anything like it before in my life.

The name of the company was Southwest Company. It's pretty well-known for turning boys into men and girls into women. Honestly, I would never want my kids to do it now, but I did it and in the process of going door-to-door I learned many lessons.

I learned that plenty of effort is required, especially at first, to get a little bit of a result. But I also learned that you gain momentum as you go. I guess I have Southwest Company to thank for starting out in business, and for what I am sharing with you now.

We need to touch on the concept of dollars per day versus dollars per job. This can be a sensitive issue, especially for people who are used to working for an hourly wage. If you get caught up in the dollars per hour, you will never achieve the level of income I earn.

Getting caught up in dollars per job is also a losing game. If you are working, you are earning. If you are sitting around playing video games, you are not earning. Playing video games while you wait for a voice over job that pays more per hour or more per job is not earning you a penny. Take the jobs and your pennies will pile up into dollars.

If you're not working right now, who cares how much the job pays? If you can fill your day, you are moving down the track. I started off trying to make $200 a day because that was a full-time income to me at the time. That would nearly have replaced my income at the time, so I thought we could survive on $200 per day. But a few months later I met that goal. And then one fine day I earned 10 times that much in one day.

If you are wondering, "What kind of jobs do I need to get?" you are on the right track. If you have started asking, "What kind of marketing plan do I need to make $500 a day?", and "What kind of clients do I need to attract?", you are way down the track, speeding along. These are the right questions to ask at any point in your voice over career, so start asking them now.

Pretty soon you will be asking, "Who are my best paying clients?". You will become focused on making sure they are happy with your work. And when the time comes, you will drop some lower paying clients to make room for higher paying clients. But you can see that it's a gradual process. You have to be working for some paying clients in order to have the privilege of dropping them for higher paying clients. You have to start somewhere.

When I suggest you drop some clients, I am not suggesting you burn bridges. I'm thankful for the relationships, but I just don't have time for everybody now because I want to make $1,000 a day. The questions I ask myself and the way I manage my time becomes completely different as I move along my voice over career track.

When you're first starting, you've got time and you need the practice, so you can start building relationships. You need work to make money, but you also need it to make contacts. Perhaps you have already figured out that my advice is to take what you can get.

Do the job, do every job, and you will begin to evolve your voice over talent and your client list. You cannot make the progress needed unless you are working. So, get work and do it well now.

Chapter 19

Database Marketing – Make Your Clients Work For You

Your database is your list of existing clients. You will also accumulate contacts for whom you have not produced work, and you will want to market to them regularly as well. But in this chapter I am talking about how to stay on the radar screen of all the clients you have worked with in the past because they are very likely to hire you again. It's just a matter of time.

Think of your database marketing as the back end of your marketing activities. The front end is new contacts you are cultivating to get work. The back end is existing clients. It's just as important to keep in touch after you produce work for a client as it was before you got the job.

Remember – it's cheaper to keep a client than it is to get a new client. Every client is money in your pocket. That is gold. And you want to treat it as precious, valuable cargo.

The data in your database is simply the person's name, the business name, the phone number, and the email and street addresses. It's all the information you need to keep in touch with a client. I like to use email quite frequently. Occasionally I like to phone call. But I need all that information on hand in order to stay in touch with people.

You will need to find a program to store the contact information easily. I use Outlook. I've worked with programs called Act and Salesforce in previous jobs, so I know those programs and I understand the value of customer relationship management (CRM) software. They fill the needs of larger organizations, but you don't need anything complex in your voice over business. You just want to keep it simple. Complex CRM software is overkill for what I do.

My advice about software for capturing all your client contact information is pretty similar to my advice about recording and editing programs – find a program you like and learn it well. The main thing is to get started building your database from the very beginning of your business. Once you have a client, capture their information and save it.

A client is any person and any company who has paid you, or will be paying you soon. Get all the contact information before you start any job so you have it handy. Personally, I also include contact information for anybody who has ever responded positively to a communication, such as a phone call or an email I sent out in my marketing efforts.

As your database grows larger, you can think about segmenting it so you send different messages to various types of clients. The ones that generate a lot of business receive an email that is worded differently than the other contacts.

My assistant helps me keep track of my income and exactly where every dollar comes from. We have a simple 3-tier system that's based on that, meaning where the dollars come from, and what needs to happen to keep them coming. This system comes in very handy for marketing.

I use this system for prioritizing my work every day, as well as for my daily, weekly and monthly marketing activities. When I can see where the dollars are coming from I know how to focus my attention, and I know which clients are slipping down towards the bottom of the list.

I may have to let some of my clients go in order to devote the time to other clients who generate more money. Of course I treat all my clients professionally, but it's only natural the ones providing me with more income will get more of my attention.

Clients who migrate toward the top of the list, on the other hand, are the ones I proactively call and email regularly. I am constantly in touch with them, one way or the other. They get top level and personalized service from me because I make a point to know their business and what they need, preferably ahead of time. I like them to know I'm on the ball and looking out for their best interests when I get in touch by phone or email.

If you don't have a marketing background, and you haven't worked in a sales job requiring you to keep a client contact list in order to make your living, some of this may be unfamiliar to you. If I sound like I'm repeating myself or beating you up with the importance of marketing, there is something you need to remember because it will make or break your voice over business.

People will not remember you. Period. They forget. They forget you if you fail to pop up and remind them who you are and what you can do for them now. That is marketing 101 in a nutshell.

You have to plan ahead, and you have to execute your plan. The goal of your marketing plan is to pop up on people's radar screens to get work. Timing is important in executing your plan, and that means knowing how much communication is just enough.

Too much communication is just as ineffective as too little because you can accidentally become an irritation. You don't want to become spam in their email inbox. You want to show up just often enough to jog their memories once in a while.

General marketing wisdom holds that you need to reach out to your contacts six times per year. But that's just an average and I don't think it is enough for voice over talent. I go for once a month, at a minimum. I do this with all the contacts in my database because it has become so fast, easy and cheap. I don't have to pay for printing and postage; I just send a group email.

When I say that I send it, actually my service sends it. I use SmartContactTool.com to generate a monthly message that is not a marketing message. Yes, this is marketing activity for me, but the subject of the email is not a sales pitch at all. It's a human interest subject, a short two or three paragraph news item.

The email says, basically, "Hey, did you see this? I thought you might find this interesting." And then I ask a question. It actually looks like I sat down to write the entire email, which I didn't, because I really don't have time to do that. I use SmartContactTool.com to do it for me and to send it on schedule once a month. That keeps me on track with my database marketing, which is my goldmine.

I've sent out a newsletter, too. A newsletter is a tool that can work well, along with phone calls and video mail. I understand many people, perhaps you are one of them, worry about the possibility of over communicating. I mentioned that possibility earlier, but it is not so great as to keep you from monthly emails.

Nobody is going to consider your monthly emails intrusive, unless they just don't ever want to hear from you again. And if that is the case, you are better off when they unsubscribe. They are doing you a favor to unsubscribe.

Let that be your biggest problem – that you over communicate to somebody to the point they unsubscribe. So, who cares? There are so many others who welcome your emails because they need to hire voice talent, and they don't mind hearing from somebody who has it together in the marketing department. You have much more to gain by constantly staying in touch with people, so don't focus on the fact that from time to time somebody will ask you to stop.

I had one thing ingrained in my head was when I was working as a consultant for a business consulting firm in Chicago. We worked with small- to medium-size businesses, and we would go back and hit those businesses every year because there would be a new staff, new people for us to deal with.

Employee turnover is a fact of business life and you have to plan for it. You have to understand there will be new people to deal with all the time. Again, don't let that stand between you and getting clients and making money. Set up your marketing plan and put it in motion to stay on the radar screens and get more business. Don't let any ideas or any excuses get in your way. Just do it.

Chapter 20

Collecting Your Money – Scoop Up Every Dollar You Earn

In the voice over business you will not get paid until you deliver your work. Some talent may be paid a part of their fee up front, but you will not be in that category when you are starting out. I never require payment up front, although I'm not saying it's wrong to do so.

Although I didn't track it until recently, I knew my collection rate was really, really high. I knew I was getting paid most of the time. But I finally sat down and did the math, and what I discovered was a 99.7% collection rate. That means I got paid for nearly all my work.

This is not always the case for voice over talent. Sometimes a client will fail to pay you, no matter how good your work is and how many times you ask them for your money. My 99.7% collection rate is very high, and so I asked myself why it's working that way for me.

I thought to myself, this is really good, but exactly why is it so good? And it boiled down to the fact that I look at every aspect of my business from a marketing standpoint. I treat my collections almost the same way I treat new contacts when I am getting a new client. Knowing that people forget about you, if you want to keep a client, if you want to get paid, you have to stay on their radar.

The fact is, if they're not thinking about you, they may not pay you. You can drop to the bottom of their payout list. I have a philosophy in my business and in my life, which is that most people intend to do the right thing. Very few clients intend to take advantage of you from the outset.

I'm not saying it can't happen or it won't happen, but if you spend all your time and energy trying to protect yourself against that occasional non-paying client, you'll end up driving others away. You will end up losing money.

Part of my philosophy about marketing and about life in general stems from my personality. I don't worry about this kind of thing. I figure if they're going to take advantage of me, they're simply going to do it. I cannot change them. I am focused on providing excellent service and making the assumption that they are going to want more of me. They know won't get more of me if they don't pay me eventually. It's that simple.

So, I treat collections as a marketing activity. And I approach it with the assumption that they intend to pay me because they will want more of my services. But sometimes a client falls on hard times. And so I don't always get paid on time, meaning within 30 days. Sometimes these things stretch out longer than I would like, of course. That is common in any business.

Mallory, my assistant, handles all my invoicing for me. She sends invoices and follows up on unpaid invoices. She stays in touch with these people. We never allow them to forget we are looking forward to serving them again.

However, if a client hasn't paid me, even if they are a couple months late, I will usually work for them. There have only been a few situations I can remember when I actually required payment prior to recording another job for a client.

Usually it's because their cash flow is tight temporarily and I'll give them the benefit of the doubt. Now, if they prove me wrong over time, I'll wait for them to pay me first. But normally I find that my patience with them and my willingness to serve them works as an excellent marketing opportunity.

Here's what I say when a client wants more work and hasn't paid me – "Say, I'd like to do this job for you. I don't know if you overlooked my last invoice, but here is a copy." We use the situation to make a good impression in order to build relationships, not destroy them. We use our collection activity to stay on their radar screens. We don't beg for it. We don't pound them to pay.

And we never, ever get nasty. Even for the most delinquent account we never get nasty because most of the time we don't need to do that. Another fact of business life is that if a client is not going to pay you, getting nasty won't help the situation at all. It never works. They are just not going to pay you, no matter what.

Nearly 100% of my clients pay me. It's actually amazing to me. If a client is overdue, on first of the month we send another copy of the invoice with a friendly reminder. It's really that simple.

If non-payment stretches past 90-120 days, then we start making phone calls and saying, "We're looking at our records. We see that you're X number of days overdue. We just wanted to find out when we could expect to receive payment." And we don't say it in an accusatory or a condescending manner. We continue to behave as though we believe they simply overlooked it.

We remain professional, friendly and persistent. Persistence in everything is my theme, in case you haven't noticed. If you don't get a job the first time you knock on the door, you keep knocking. You just keep on knocking.

As you keep knocking you will find those doors will eventually open. You don't want to be forgotten. That's the key to all your marketing, which includes collections. Don't allow yourself to be forgotten.

Chapter 21

How I Set My Rates

Honestly, it's the Wild, Wild West out there in terms of voice over rates. They're all over the place and for good reason. The reason is that voice over jobs vary so much. There are a few factors to consider when considering rates, and they will serve to guide you as you venture into the Wild, Wild West.

You need to know if a job will be used for broadcast, non-broadcast, internal or external use. You need to know what kind of audience will hear your work in order to know how much to charge for your work.

The size of the potential listening audience is a factor, as is the size of the client. If you're working for a small market radio station, producing a commercial for Bob's Used Cars, it will not pay you as much as a national commercial for K-Mart. It is a big mistake to expect to be paid a certain hourly rate by any and all clients because the business just doesn't work that way.

Sadly, voice over talent often approach all jobs the same way. They say, "This is my rate." And that's that. Maybe that's that in their own minds, but in the real world it's not that way at all. Local jobs simply don't pay as much as national jobs.

You have to understand this reality when you work as voice talent. You ultimately don't determine the rate you are paid. The market will always determine the rate. In other words, you can say whatever you want, but the client gets to accept or reject your offer. You won't have final control over the pay rate.

If I can determine a client's budget, that's where I like to start. I always think it's best to get the client to show you their hand first because it may be far less than you expect. Or, it may be far more.

Let's say I get a call like this one – "Hey, Bill, we're thinking of producing this commercial for a local business with five stores, most of them in Ohio. One or two are in Kentucky. And I just wanted to get an idea of what this might cost."

My first response will be – "How many commercials do you want? What's the length of the project?" And I may hear - "These are 60-second spots. They're going to run on radio. We've got a campaign mapped out for the next six weeks for all six stores."

Then I'll say, "Do you want this to be a buy-out? In other words, do you want to own this?" That means they will pay me once and will not owe me any more money in the form of residuals, no matter how many times the commercials are aired. I usually hear – "We don't want pay for it more than once."

My next question would be ¬– "Do you have a budget in place for voice over talent for this project?" And, naturally, I often hear, "We want to pay as little as possible." To which I reply, "When you say that, do you have an idea how much it might be?" And then, unfortunately, I may hear – "You know, we haven't really done much of this before so I don't know exactly."

When I get to that point with a client, he's just not going to tell me his budget. So, that's when I have to come up with a dollar amount for him. I have to know how much I need to charge because I'm going to go first in this price negotiation and I don't want to turn it into a game. I don't have time to keep going back and forth whenever a client won't make the first offer.

So, I'll throw out a number. I'm computing in my head, and sometimes I blurt out a price too quickly. To avoid regret, I've learned to ask more questions before making an offer. I try to gather as much information as possible, including scripts.

So, at this point I might say, "Would you mind sending me the script and the information you just gave me over the telephone? I'd like to take a look at it and get a better idea of what the script is like and then I'll give you a quote." This question saves me blurting out a price that's too low because I made some assumptions about the project that were just plain wrong.

I can't tell you how many times I've assumed something about a script or a project and then once I saw it I wished I'd asked more questions before giving a price. This scenario doesn't usually happen with commercials, but with long narration. I might receive the script and discover that it includes heavy medical terminology.

In that case, I will have to spend time learning to pronounce medical terms before I can record, which takes a considerable amount of time. Some narration for training videos can easily take five times longer than normal narration.

Learning new vocabulary is very time consuming and I have learned to include my study time in my pricing. Occasionally I'm surprised by how simple a script I receive, but that is rare.

If I hear this – "We don't have a script yet.", then I have to make a decision. If I respond by asking him to send the script when it's available, he'll usually call somebody else for the job. So, at this point I may give him a price.

I have a rate sheet that I don't send out unless it's absolutely necessary, and I might pull it out and send it. Or, I may say, "I would typically charge $500 or $600." And then I'll wait for him to respond. That number is the beginning of our negotiation process.

As I said, I'm not big into playing games. I'm not desperate for the money, and even back when I was desperate, I never played desperate. I like to work with people who are easy to work with and if he starts trying to lowball me, I won't play very long. I have too much work already.

Keep this fact in mind, once again, in order to make decisions in your marketing and negotiating activities: there is plenty of work out there. It's time-consuming to find the jobs, but there's a lot of voice over work available. Your voice over career does not ride on any one job. And most of the time you will hear some numbers when you ask for a project budget.

They'll tell you the price range they have budgeted for voice over, which is normally $150 to $200, or $250 to $300, or $700 to $800. It's usually a very tight range at any level. And, the truth is I may have a number in my mind already. If my number is on the lower end of their offer, then I'll accept the lower end. If it's on the higher end of their offer, I may say I was hoping for $400.

Here's a good example of what I might say to get the client in order to build my business – "You know what, I would typically charge a little bit more, but this time around, since we haven't worked together and I'd like the opportunity to show you what I can do, I can do it for $300, just this time." That offer leaves the door open to charge a higher rate in the future. You have done the client a favor and you have acquired a new client, so you both win.

You may be getting the impression I'm having these conversations with a client on the phone. That can happen, but more often they occur by email, and they are emails sent by my assistant as she checks with me for the appropriate response. Most of my negotiating is done through emails while Mallory and I are having a discussion. She reads all my email and she'll tell me who has contacted me and what they want.

Many times Mallory has already asked for the script. If not, I'll suggest she ask for the script or whatever I want her to say. We almost have templates for these exchanges because we've done them so many times, and she usually knows exactly what I'm going to say. Ninety-nine out of a 100 negotiations are handled through emails.

Remember that your rate is not your only negotiating tool. Turnaround time is a big negotiating tool as well. I don't want to appear to be too terribly easy to work with because that gives the impression I am not busy.

If a budget is lower than what I would typically charge for a similar type of project, I might say, "Okay, you know I can work with that if you can give me X number of days to get it done." That is how I make sure they know I'm busy and a successful voice talent.

This way, I get a job on my schedule and I also get a new client who respects me. I very frequently use that sentence as a negotiating tool. However, if you are a union member the rates have been determined by the union and you will work within the specified time frame. You will not have options to negotiate your rate. If you are non-union then you must develop a good feel for where you will begin your negotiating process on your own behalf.

You can go the website of SAG-AFTRA to see published rates, which will give you a starting point. When I do that, I know my rates will need to be lower than published union rates. But my goal is to charge as much as possible. Non-union jobs for clients with smaller budgets pay less for voice over talent. That's a given.

If you can charge half of the published union rate, that's generally pretty good. I mean, it's not bad money and it does not represent a desperate concession on your part. It is commercially viable, as they say. It is what the marketplace will bear because non-union jobs are lower paying jobs, and there are a lot more non-union jobs available.

I'll take $200 a spot for local commercials all day long. Give me five of those every day. That makes my job really easy. It meets my goal of $1,000 per day right now, and it satisfies repeat clients who will provide more jobs and more money for me on a continuing basis. I am a working voice over talent and that means I will choose to work because I choose to earn an income everyday. No work = no income. I choose to work.

Chapter 22

Your World-Class Customer Service

When you hear the term "customer service" you might not immediately think of it as a marketing activity, but it is. It's a huge, powerful marketing activity, because it's far easier and cheaper to keep a client than it is to go out and get a new client.

So, when you get good clients you need to do everything in your power to retain them and make them happy. If you have a good client, you want to keep it. A good client is one that is easy to work with and pays you on time. A good client makes your job and your life easy, so that's what you need to offer in return. Or, in many cases, you need to be very cooperative long before the job begins.

Here's the thing you have to keep in mind - you are a commodity. You have to think about yourself this way in order to survive. Voice over talent is easy to find, so it's very easy to get a substitute for you. There are thousands of other people waiting to take the job that I don't take, or work with the client I lose. There are thousands waiting in the wings.

I know this very well and I structure my business around this fact, as well as the fact that even my clients will forget about me unless I pop up on their radar screens. It is in my own best interest to do everything in my power to keep clients I like, and clients who pay me. The thing that separates struggling voice over talent from successful voice over talent is getting and keeping good clients.

Sometimes I ask my clients, "Why do you use me?" That question might sound funny, but it always provides me with useful information that I appreciate. I want to hear their replies so I can keep doing the right things. The thing that absolutely amazes me is the answer I hear most often. I'll bet it will amaze you, too.

Over and over I hear clients say it is hard to find people who do what they say they will do. That is exactly what I hear from clients. Sometimes they tell me I did a great job, too, and I always appreciate that.

But what I hear more often is simply that I did the job, I did it on time, and I communicated with them during the job. I do not hear them say it's because I have such a great voice. That doesn't happen.

What they'll say is, "Not only do you do good work, but you get stuff done on time and you do what you say you're going to do and you communicate with us." Honestly, this comment shocked me when I first heard it because I thought everybody has to do these things in order to compete.

I thought all the voice talent out there cares as much about keeping customers as I do. But the amazing thing is, they don't. I call this amazing quality The X Factor. If you have The X Factor, it will differentiate you from all the other thousands of voice talent who have similar voice skills, but no customer service skills. Other people may be every bit as good a voice over talent as you are, or even better, but if you can serve your customer better they will hire you instead.

Eliminate their constant hassles with flaky talent and you will rise above the crowd. You will become their go-to person. You will be the one making money and not the person who flaked out on the client.

I'm talking about the most basic things here. I'm not talking about anything complicated or sophisticated. I'm talking about communicating and performing the job in a timely manner.

When I get an email inquiring whether I'm available for a job, I always respond within a few hours. They get my answer quickly. If they ask if I can complete a job by tomorrow, and I agree to complete it for them, they will get it tomorrow. I will do whatever it takes to do what I say I will do. If I can't do it by tomorrow, then I'm honest and I let them know up front.

This is how they know they can trust me. I've got clients who come back to me again and again, simply because I get their project done when I say I'm going to get it done. It's that simple. I may be a commodity, but apparently my prompt service is competitive advantage in the voice over business.

I was shocked to discover it's not that difficult to rise above the crowd once you get an opportunity to do so. It is work, but it is do-able. It's not rocket science or brain surgery. It's just a matter of keeping your word and staying in touch with people.

I have two teenage sons I am trying to teach this important lesson. So, I contribute a certain amount of dollars per month to the purchase and upkeep of a car they both use, but I also have made a requirement for each of them.

I told them both to pay me X number of dollars per month, and that way both of them contribute toward the purchase and the upkeep of the vehicle. I contribute approximately one-third of the total. Both my sons are very agreeable to this arrangement.

Sometimes they cannot pay me on the first of every month as we've agreed, so they need to alert me and explain their situation. I believe it's not the end of the world if a person can't always perform on time, but I tell them they absolutely need to let me know. I am trying to teach my sons not to flake out. I guess some parents don't manage to teach this important lesson to their kids.

And I hate to say it, since you can see my personal take on the issue, but the fact that most voice over talent doesn't choose to perform on time and keep in close touch during production actually works in your favor if you choose to do both those simple things. Most clients will work with you if there's a legitimate delay, but when you flake out and quit communicating people write you off.

It also happens when you don't follow through. Keep your word, follow through and fix what needs to be fixed. Don't make things difficult for your clients; make things easy for them. Make it easy for clients to work with you.

I don't ask for money up front because it's a hurdle the client has to jump. Avoid creating hurdles. I generally ask for payment upon completion, and I also provide a little guarantee. I tell them if they don't like it, they don't have to pay me. That's never happened, by the way.

If a client actually thought my work was inadequate I would not expect payment for it. If they don't like it, they don't have to use it. But if they like it, and it's what they asked for, then you can see that most will pay me. As I said, 99.7% of my clients pay me.

All this being said, some clients are simply not worth the trouble it takes to keep them. You have to know when to fire bad clients. When I say bad clients, I am talking about clients who do not enhance my ROI, my return on investment.

I always consider what I am getting from a relationship in comparison to what I am giving to it. I've had clients who became such a hassle it was just not cost effective to work with them. Their demands exceeded their value to me.

You get to decide who is worth working with and who is not. You are self-employed; this is your voice over business. You don't need to become miserable doing it. And, frankly, there's enough work out there that you don't need to keep every client.

Never feel you can't turn down a job, politely of course. Thanks, but no thanks. You can say, "I don't want to work for you anymore." I've said it on several occasions when it was no longer worth the hassle, financially or emotionally.

You'll discover some clients are extremely easy to work with, too. Those will become your favorite clients. But with some, the demands never end. You can never completely satisfy them. They are just hard to work with, and they take up too much time to add to your ROI, the overall value of your voice over business. When you are building a six figure voice over business, you have to consider and defer to your ROI. It matters. You matter.

Whenever a client drains you physically and emotionally it is time to let them go. Then you can spend your time marketing to pick up some new clients. Make room for your ROI to grow by freeing yourself from draining clients, even if it is difficult the first time. Soon you will see the wisdom in this suggestion.

Chapter 23

A Few More Things
To Know Before We Go

As you can see, I don't believe in fluff or filler. I only am concerned with doing things and being involved in activities that produce results and profit. Hopefully, I've achieved those goals in this book.

I have written this book to explain how to do things, why to do them, and what you can expect when you do them. You can expect results that produce profit in your voice over business.

It's a matter of taking the simple tools we've outlined and executing them. That's where people generally fail. They get all excited at first, and then they fail to follow through. They are not prepared to endure the monotony, the grind.

I've used those words before, but I'm using them again to make a serious point. If you think voice over is a glamorous occupation 365 days a year, you're mistaken. It's not. It's a job and it is hard work. Some days it is a monotonous grind.

I think you'd be hard pressed to find a job that doesn't fit that description, however. Even most jobs you might consider to be glamorous are not always that way. There's always the grind, the tedious, repetitive activity that must go on to build a business and achieve success.

Don't misunderstand me here, I love this career. I thoroughly enjoy doing what it takes to build my six figure voice over business. I get a thrill when I complete a project and people all over the country hear my work.

When people ask me if it was my voice they heard on radio or television, I love to say, "Yeah, that was me." It's a kick to hear that. It's fun to be recognized by my voice over work.

But for one ounce of fame, there will be tons and tons of basic hard work involved. There are spikes on the screen to edit and cold calls to make. There are negotiations to answer and clients to juggle. To me, it's all fun because it keeps me behind the microphone. I love being behind a microphone, so I do whatever it takes to stay there.

Now you've read my book and you know what I have to say about the voice over business. If you can grasp the basic principles I've shared, and you are willing to run with them, to follow them relentlessly, you will succeed in building your own voice over business, too. You know what I know, and now you need to do what I do. That's all. Now, go do it!

Resources

The Voice Over Playbook
www.VoiceOverPlaybook.com
The ultimate voice over marketing resource. This 4 hour streaming video tutorial is a comprehensive voice over marketing plan to take you from zero to 6 figure income as quickly as possible. It covers everything from branding yourself, to who to contact to get work, to what to say to get the job.

Voice Over Playbook Workshop (streaming video of live event)
www.VoiceOverPlaybookWorkshop.com
The Voice Over Playbook Workshop is a full day event held in a small group setting. The is a streaming video of the seminar based on the original "Voice Over Playbook!" This event covers the A-Z of marketing your voice over business and growing it into a substantial and sustainable income.

To learn more about and register for Bill's next Voice Over Playbook event:
wwwVoiceOverPlaybookSeminar.com

Audio Book Success Seminar (streaming video of live event)
www.AudiobookSuccess2.com
This is a recording of Bill's 2-day live audiobook seminar event. This workshop is held in a small group setting with lots of interaction and Q&A . Topics such as "How to Select Your Niche," "How to Give Your Best Read," and "How to Market Yourself as an Audiobook Narrator" are covered. Bonus footage of Bill directing talent during recording sessions is provided to help you better understand the art of audiobook narration.

To learn more about and register for Bill's next Audiobook Seminar event:
www.AudiobookSeminar.com

Answers to the Top 100 Voice Over Questions
www.100VOQuestions.com
Bill receives questions from aspiring (as well as seasoned) voice over talent on a daily basis. He has complied the top 100 and provided answers in streaming video for you to access anytime/anywhere. This is an incredible resource to get fast an-

swers to your most important and burning voice over related question.

Voice Over Demo Secrets
www.VoiceOverDemoSecrets.com
In addition to being a very successful voice talent, Bill is also a highly sought after voice over demo producer. Did you that your voice over demo, more than any other single thing, will determine whether agents, casting directors, and clients will even give you serious consideration? In this audio program learn the secrets to demo production that will unlock the doors to more work and less frustration.

Voice Over Fast Track
www.VoiceOverFastTrack.com
If you're new to voice overs (or you need a solid refresher program) than this is the course for you! This 4 week small group tele-course is designed to cover everything you need to know from A-Z. It will help get you up and running quickly and. Creating a home studio, recording your demo, voice over niches, read styles, marketing your business and more will be covered. A lot of time is given to practicing reads and getting feedback directly from Bill.

Voice Over Group Coaching
www.VOGroupCoaching.com
This is live group coaching with Bill DeWees. This is a small group format allowing interaction and lots of personal attention. The group format is a platform to share ideas and receive expert coaching and strategies.

Speaker to Voice Talent
www.SpeakerToVoiceTalent.com
If you are a public speaker and want to turn "down time" into profit, this audio program is for you!

For 1 on 1 coaching with Bill visit www.VoiceTalentCoach.com

For over 100 FREE video tutorials, visit Bill's YouTube channel at www.YouTube.com/user/VoiceOverExpert

FREE OFFER

FREE OFFER for YOU as the owner of this book!

To get my audio program "Seven Secrets to a 6 Figure Voice Over Income"

Just go to: http://goo.gl/U1STb

You can download it RIGHT NOW!

What are you waiting for????

FREE OFFER

43584862R00082

Made in the USA
Middletown, DE
26 April 2019